HOW TO STRETCH YOUR DOLLAR

BY ADELE WHITELY FLETCHER

A Benjamin Company/Rutledge Book
New York

SBN 87502-001-1

Library of Congress Catalog Card Number 68-26766
Copyright © 1968 by
The Benjamin Company, Inc. and Rutledge Books, Inc.
Published by
The Benjamin Company, Inc.
485 Madison Avenue
New York, N.Y. 10022
and by
Rutledge Books, Inc.
17 East 45th Street
New York, N.Y. 10017
Printed in the United States of America

PREFACE

The dollar isn't what it used to be. Prices have been climbing steadily over many years and recently have spiraled to an all-time high.

You have fewer dollars to spend. Tax increases—Federal, state and city—have come on top of "hidden" taxes in the cost of your gasoline, entertainment, cosmetics, cigarettes and hundreds of other items.

Income has gone up—fortunately! But not always as much as prices, taxes—and your desires. Today you need many expensive items—from appliances to education—that you did not even want yesterday.

How can you stretch your dollar? Simply by learning better dollar management, the techniques that make every dollar work harder for you.

You stretch your dollar when you know more about how manufacturers sell. For example: a lipstick made by a prestige cosmetics house can be bought—under a different name and with different packaging—in many variety stores at about one quarter of the luxury price.

A combination washing machine and dryer that carries the name of a large chain mail order house sells for about $100 less than it costs under the same manufacturer's prestige trademark.

You stretch dollars when you know food values. A knowledgeable steak-eating family switches to flank steak because it is about 30 cents a pound cheaper than sirloin or porterhouse—and it has no bone. Properly prepared, it's tender and some feel it's tastier. It's known, incidentally, as London Broil in restaurants and hotels.

You can stretch dollars if you are imaginative. For instance, families in one neighborhood arranged to buy an extension ladder, lawn mower and other garden equipment as a group. They share the use and divide the cost.

Even if your family's income is high enough to absorb the current climb in prices and taxes, you want full value for every dollar. A knowledgeable approach to spending puts us on a firm footing. It underwrites the building of a happy, successful family life.

Dollar-stretching can be fun. It always brings a sense of accomplishment and satisfaction. It influences young children to spend their money intelligently.

Every financial expert agrees that you don't need genius or born talent to make dollars do more. It's through *learning* that you find the simple, practical and effective ways to get a dollar's worth—even a dollar and five cents' worth—for every dollar you spend. You *learn* how to avoid buying mistakes, to sidestep the cheats and frauds.

The chapters that follow tell you the simple techniques. They are up-to-date. They will stretch your dollar when you shop for food, clothing . . . run your car . . . maintain your house, rent your apartment . . . go on vacation or take out family insurance. They will help you to save and give you sound advice about investment.

Everyone can learn more about managing those dollars. Whatever your income, this handbook will make them work much harder—for you.

CONTENTS

Chapter One

MORE
FOR YOUR
MONEY

The Clark family and the Peterson family have about the same annual income. They each have three children. They live in areas where goods and services are comparably priced. But here the similarity ends.

The Clarks own their own home. It has labor-saving appliances and is attractively furnished. Their one major debt is the mortgage payments on the house, but they are building equity. The special savings account they opened for their children's college education is growing. They get out for a night on the town often enough to keep Mrs. Clark from feeling like a household drudge. The family manages a vacation every summer. The Clarks lead an optimistic life.

The Petersons are in debt. Because they cannot get a decent mortgage they rent an apartment, paying out month after month and getting no equity. After 11 years of marriage their home is not fully furnished. Mrs. Peterson has a clothes washer but no dryer, and her refrigerator and range are vintage models. If the Peterson children are not accepted by the tuition-free state university, they will have to go to work. Ninety percent of the dissension in the Peterson home revolves around one thing: money.

Where have the Petersons gone wrong? Where have the Clarks done right? The Clarks are simply smart consumers and dollar-stretchers.

Like the Clarks, you can stretch your dollars, buy more

things and lead a more comfortable, rewarding life by following a few basic principles. Know precisely how much you have to spend during the entire year; always decide what you will buy before you go out to shop, taking into account your annual budget; buy only what you want and need, never on impulse or because a salesman pressures you; become an expert on how products function, and which one gives you the best value for your money; learn which stores give you the lowest cost, and when and where sales are held; and avoid misleading contracts and overdependence on credit.

What can you spend?

Ask most people how much they can spend annually, and they answer with the yearly salary of the breadwinner. But this is the gross figure and it can be misleading. What you need to know is the *net* figure—what is left after Federal and state withholding taxes, after hospitalization and insurance premiums, social security payments, union dues and other fixed charges you may have.

On the other hand, don't underestimate your spending power. Include your husband's Christmas bonus (if you are sure of it), interest from savings accounts and any dividend payments if you own stock.

How much of your yearly income you spend on various goods and services depends partly on how you and your family like to live. If you'd rather buy new carpeting this year instead of taking a vacation, fine—as long as you know that you can't manage both. If buying a freezer means you can save money by stocking up food during sales, then such an expense may be right for you.

In buying, nothing is absolutely "right" or "wrong" so long as you can afford it and get the most for your dollars. But as a guide, here is how the average American family spends, according to a report based on statistics from the Bureau of Labor:

 • Food consumes 24 percent of the average family's annual expenditures.

● Rent, mortgage payments, home insurance, property taxes, home maintenance and improvement also account for 24 percent.

● Transportation—the family car, auto insurance, commuting to work, long-distance travel—takes 15 percent.

● Another 10 percent is spent on clothing and shoes.

● About 9½ percent goes for medical insurance, doctor and dentist bills, drugs and medicines, plus personal care items such as haircuts, beauty salons and cosmetics.

● Household furnishings, appliances and other equipment account for 5 percent.

● About 3½ percent is spent on alcohol and tobacco, 4 percent on recreation, 2 percent on reading material and education and another 2 percent on all other expenditures—including gifts, life insurance, charitable contributions and interests on loans.

Plan before you buy

Merchants estimate that as much as 70 percent of their goods are bought on impulse. How many of these wind up on a closet shelf after a single use or two? Advance planning—deciding what you need and want—will help you to avoid buying what you really don't need. You'll have time to learn how products function and to comparison-shop the different makes.

But comparison-shopping for certain products is just the beginning. How would you feel if you bought an expensive item only to find that another store is selling it at a lower price? Cheated, of course. You will never know where the best values are unless you take the time to comparison-shop the various stores.

Investigate the different types—department stores, discount houses, clearance centers, specialty stores, secondhand shops. Then comparison-shop *within* each type. One discount house, for example, may offer truer discounts than its competitors.

Also check out departments with similar merchandise

within a single store. Buyers often try to outdo each other and you may do better at a sale in a store's high-priced department than you would buying the regular stock in the budget shop.

Here is a brief description of dollar-stretching possibilities in different kinds of stores:

Discount stores can save you a great deal, especially on big-ticket items, and are worth the time and energy you spend on them. But decide beforehand on the brand you want. Some manufacturers rent space in a discount house and set up a salesman to get you to buy his product. If you know what you want in advance, you can avoid being swayed.

Some discount houses discourage returns or exchanges by making them time-consuming and inconvenient for the customer. No law requires a dealer or store to exchange merchandise or accept returns. When you know what you want before you buy, you can keep your returns and exchanges down.

Department stores usually take higher markups than discount houses. Still, you can find wonderful buys at department store sales.

Most department stores take telephone orders, deliver merchandise without charge and pick up items you want to return. But although these services are offered to earn your goodwill, remember that the costs are included in the store's normal percentage of markup.

Clearance centers are usually located outside city limits where rent and overhead are lower. They serve as outlets for store and manufacturer leftover stock, and they offer exceptional savings, particularly in furniture, bedding and carpeting. Clearance centers are essentially self-service, and you may have to arrange for your own delivery.

Bargain basements are found in most department stores. Sometimes the merchandise there comes from the same manufacturers who supply the upper floors with higher-priced items. Bargain basements may also serve as a store's general clearing house. If you've been eying an item you can't afford upstairs, check occasionally to see if it has been sent down with a reduced price tag.

Thrift shops and resale stores sell used merchandise, and you can sometimes pick up a very attractive item for an unbelievably low price. Thrift shops sell clothing, furniture, glassware, jewelry, silver, books, paintings, china and just about anything else you might want.

Secondhand stores dealing in furniture offer especially great bargains. The dealers haunt country auctions and raid attics to find handsome old Victorian pieces and other cast-offs. Some will strip and refinish the furniture for you—for a price, of course. But you can do it yourself. Any good paint store has the materials you need, plus advice on how to go about it.

Auctions may offer anything from priceless furniture to paperback books. A day or two is usually set aside before the sale so that buyers can see the merchandise at leisure and, if necessary, bring an expert to appraise items. Be sure you know the value of any item before you bid, or you may pay more for it at an auction than you would someplace else.

Used merchandise from private owners may be your best buy of all. Furniture bought from a family that is moving far away and doesn't want to pay for shipping, or a complete wardrobe from a woman who has lost or gained a great deal of weight, can sometimes be bought for almost nothing. Watch the merchandise-for-sale ads in your local newspaper. Be sure the sell-off is legitimate and not a blind for a regular business.

Should you buy for credit or cash?

Very few of us would own houses or cars if we had to wait until we had the full purchase price in cash. An intelligent use of credit might enable you to have a few more possessions. But a foolhardy use of credit can plunge you into debt so that you will actually have fewer things, little money in the bank and a lot of heartache.

There are many advantages to buying for cash. You

cannot spend more than you have. Sudden hardship—the loss of a job, or medical expenses—will not find you with a lot of bills you cannot pay. When you save for a large item in a savings account, the money earns interest. Then you can buy wherever you get the best price, not only in stores where you have charge accounts.

There are also real advantages to an intelligent use of credit, and once you establish a good credit rating, you will be able to get additional credit in a sudden emergency.

But there are many kinds of credit. Which type is better suited to your overall dollar-stretching?

Regular charge accounts, offered as a rule only in certain department stores and specialty shops, require no down payment or prepurchase deposit. The customer pays nothing on a purchase for at least 30 days. A bill that goes unpaid much beyond that time may be taxed a carrying charge.

90-day accounts, offered mainly by specialty shops and a few department stores, permit the bill to be paid in three monthly installments, without interest charges.

Revolving charge accounts permit you to charge, in one month or with a single purchase, up to a maximum amount the store has allocated to you. The account is payable in monthly installments, and no interest is charged if the bill is paid in full when rendered. But otherwise interest of 1½ percent monthly or 18 percent annually is the rule.

Charge credit plans place no ceiling on the amount of credit and call for small monthly payments. On the first of any month in which you make a new purchase, a bonus payment is required. There is an interest charge on the balance of 1½ percent monthly—or 18 percent a year.

Short-term plans or installment credit make it possible for expensive items such as major appliances and furniture to be paid for in monthly installments. The carrying charges on accounts of this kind may include interest rates ranging from 1½ percent or 3½ percent monthly to 40 percent annually, and that's a lot. Before you sign any short-term plan or installment agreement, check to see whether it would be more economical to use a savings account loan, negotiate one from a thrift institution — or to pay cash.

Credit cards are now held by millions of Americans and can be used for charging anything from a meal in a restaurant to a new dress or a trip around the world. Most cards can be obtained for a fee of $10, and another $10 a year. The stores that want your business pay the credit card company about seven percent of everything their card-carrying customers charge. They tend to raise their prices by about seven percent, too.

Before you sign any contract

To sign a contract without first reading and understanding its terms is as dangerous and foolish as signing a blank check. A contract sets down the mutual obligations of the seller and the buyer. The wording will protect the seller. Make certain it also protects you, the buyer. A signed contract cannot be altered or canceled without the written permission of the seller, even if you return or refuse to accept the merchandise. Pay particular attention to what it says about the finance charges.

The various items involved in a finance charge can be obscure. Insist that interest rates, insurance fees or any other part of the total financing arrangement be itemized separately, so that you see what you're paying for. If the terms seem too complicated or vague, ask a lawyer to check them out.

Some financing contracts contain "balloon clauses"—a series of small payments to be followed by a large sum that ends the indebtedness. Not all of these contracts bother to mention the large final sum in so many dollars and cents. Make it your business to find out.

Unscrupulous salesmen sometimes ask for a buyer's signature on what they call a "receipt for an on-trial loan." Make sure that what you're signing is not, in fact, a purchase contract instead.

Guarantees and warranties

A guarantee or warranty on a product means some protection for you. But never buy because the salesman says it is "guaranteed." Just what does the guarantee promise? Find out:

What is the guarantee's duration? Does it cover the whole item or merely some of its parts? Are there any stipulations as to the upkeep and the way the article should be used or cleaned? Can the product be returned to the store or dealer for repair and replacement, or must you send it to the manufacturer? Must you pay anything toward the cost of repairs—either parts or labor?

Always fill out the customer's part of the agreement; sign and mail it to the manufacturer in complete accordance with instructions. But remember that a guarantee or warranty—like any promise or contract—is worth no more than the integrity of the manufacturer or seller.

When a bargain isn't a bargain

A "bargain" isn't necessarily a bargain just because a store or dealer calls it one. For example, "as is" written on a ticket means that the merchandise is damaged, shopworn or defective in some way. You pay much less than the original price, but you can't return it if you decide you don't want it after all. A dented case won't affect a vacuum cleaner's performance, but a kink in the motor is something else again.

"Sold at wholesale cost" is something retail stores can rarely afford. Most so-called "wholesale" offers present some savings, but not as much as the retailer would have you believe.

Going-out-of-business sales, if genuine, can get you fabulous bargains. Unfortunately, many of them are not genuine. The merchants, when their short-term leases expire, rent another store for another month or two and exploit a similar "sale."

A reputable merchant, really liquidating, offers his stock at greatly reduced prices. Even here, take care. If your purchase turns out to be unsatisfactory or the item defective, the store owner may be out of business, and you will have no recourse.

Buy at the true sales

Most sales, however, are legitimate, and one of the biggest advantages of advance planning is that you can take advantage of sales throughout the year. These sales can save you from ten to 50 percent on just about every kind of personal or household item you can name. If you know what you want, you can stock up when the price is right.

For example, gifts for special occasions—graduation, holidays, birthdays—can be picked up during sales and stored, rather than bought at the height of the buying season when prices soar. Father's favorite after-shave lotion will smell as sweet whether you buy it during a January clearance or the week before Father's Day.

Make a list of household staples—towels, bedding, dishes, etc.—that will need filling in or replacing within the next few months. Keep a list of the gifts you'll be giving during the year. Make a calendar of the sales coming up.

It is easy to plan on sales in advance because most are held annually at specific times. Department stores generally notify their charge account customers of a sale by mail before announcing it to the general public in newspaper ads. But you will still find plenty of bargains if you get to the store soon after the ad appears.

After-Christmas sales. January is a windfall month for bargain hunters. Christmas cards, wrappings and decorations—usually marked down to half-price or less immediately after the holiday—can be bought and used the following year.

Most stores drastically mark down lingerie, toys, handbags, sweaters, gloves, toiletries and other gift items they stocked up on heavily for the holiday rush, to make room for their spring merchandise. You can buy ahead at the low prices both for your personal needs and for next Christmas' gifts. A merchant who took a higher than usual markup before Christmas—as some do—can afford to reduce his leftover merchandise to almost its wholesale price, at no loss to him and plenty of savings to you.

Clearances. Store-wide clearances and pre-inventory sales, usually held in January and July, are the stores' way of getting rid of odds and ends. You can often get anything from stockings to heavy appliances at big savings.

Store anniversaries. Many people don't realize that anniversary sales can offer excellent buys. The store plans for them months ahead by searching out attractively priced items. It alerts manufacturers with whom it does business. The manufacturers compete to support the store, reducing their prices and offering special items. They know that if they fail a store's buyer at this time they will lose goodwill or even the store's future patronage. You, the customer, can come out ahead.

Loss leaders. Here, one item or a few are marked way down and advertised to get people into the store and expose them to impulse buying that will make up for the loss leader. If something you want is featured in such a sale, go in and buy it and walk right out again.

Sales of seconds. You can save a lot of money—especially on bedding and towels—at sales of "seconds" or "irregulars" held from time to time throughout the year. Seconds are available when a manufacturer decides not to sell at his regular price because tiny flaws might damage the prestige brand name he has promoted heavily with his advertising.

These items do have imperfections, but you usually need an eagle eye to spot them and they do not affect use or durability.

Floor sample sales. Furniture and rugs used in store displays are often sold way below the original cost. So is clothing shown on mannequins or worn by models at store fashion shows. Appliances used for demonstrations can be good buys, but make sure they haven't already gotten too much wear and tear from handling in the store.

Special purchases. Special purchase sales are exactly

General Annual Sales Calendar

JANUARY
Lingerie, toys, rugs, bags, sweaters, shoes, handkerchiefs, furs, men's ties, furniture, decorations, bedding, giftwares, linens, paper wrappings—
up to 50% off

FEBRUARY
White sales in some stores; furniture, rugs in some stores—
25% to 35% off

MARCH
Check your local papers: any anniversary sales or stocking sales?
10% to 25% off

APRIL
Any special purchase sales announced in your local papers?
10% to 20% off

MAY
Women's spring suit and coat clearances—
up to 50% off

JUNE
Drastic clearances of women's spring dresses, suits and coats—
up to 75% off

JULY
Handbags—**50% and more off;** women's summer clothes and shoes—**up to 50% off;** rugs— look for remnant sales!

AUGUST
Furs, white sales—**25% to 35% off;** summer clothes clearances—**50% and more off**

SEPTEMBER
Any departmental or pre-inventory sales or special purchase sales? Check local papers—**15% off**

OCTOBER
Automobiles, coats for men and women; check local papers for toiletry sales—**25% off**

NOVEMBER
Coats for men and women; check local papers for close-out sales—
20% to 60% off

DECEMBER
(after Christmas) Lingerie, toys, men's ties, women's bags, sweaters, giftwraps, decorations, ribbons, handkerchiefs, Christmas cards—
50% off

that: the store has acquired merchandise at a special low price and is passing the saving—or at least part of it—along to you in order to have a sale. Sometimes a store and manufacturer contract for special merchandise in the hopes that the bargains will bring you into the store. Your savings average 15 percent.

Sometimes, too, a retail store acquires a full stock of merchandise from a manufacturer who sold below cost in order to free himself from financial disaster. You can expect savings of from 25 to 60 percent.

Regular department sales. Department stores regularly hold twice-a-year sales in most departments. You can stock up on virtually everything at great savings. Keep a record of when you can buy your favorite brands at these special low prices. If you need china, luggage, books or drugs during the year, find out what month they are put on sale at the stores where you like to shop.

For instance, white sales—generally held in August and again in January or February—offer good buys in sheets, pillowcases, pillows, towels, bath mats, shower curtains, tablecloths and kitchen and bathroom accessories. You can save from one-quarter to one-third of the usual cost.

Toiletry and cosmetics sales, held twice annually by most department stores, can net you savings as high as 50 percent. Sales of discontinued items are frequent in cosmetics and can mean bigger bargains yet.

POINTS TO REMEMBER

1. Become a smart consumer by planning your purchases in advance of your needs, never buying on impulse.

2. Paying cash can be an advantage, but know the intelligent use of credit. Try to buy medium-sized items for cash.

3. Study sales contracts, guarantees and warranties, their limitations and pitfalls. Read before you sign.

4. Buy at sales, held in many stores throughout the year and offering anything from handkerchiefs to furniture. In some instances, your savings will amount to 50 percent and over.

Chapter Two

YOUR FOOD DOLLAR

Food dollars go out in small amounts—39 cents here and 49 cents there—but day in and day out, a penny here and a penny there, they can add up to almost 30 percent of your income. You can cut that percentage down when you know your nutrition.

Those fancy cookbooks are fun to read. But you will save dollars and probably eat better if you invest in (1) a good book on nutrition, and (2) a basic, down-to-earth cookbook that you use every day. Spend a few hours browsing in your local public library to find the books that will be most useful to you.

Shopping know-how is your biggest dollar-saver.

Start by learning the strong points or weak departments of all the supermarkets in your area. Shop them all, at least at first, so that you can compare their offerings and prices. You may find, for instance, that one has especially good fruits and vegetables at low prices, while another offers better cuts and prices on meats. When you want to lay in a large supply of produce or meats, use the supermarket that does the most for you.

Plan your menus by the week. But before you plan, make it a habit to read all the store ads in your daily newspaper. Look for the specials. These will be the foods that are in season—plentiful and at their lowest cost. They will also be the store's loss leaders—items marked down to bring you in.

Local television and radio stations announce them as well.

Plan your menus around these specials. Whenever you can, buy them up in as much bulk as you can store at home and use up before any spoilage occurs.

Do those multiple-unit sales promoted in the store tempt you? It always pays to do your arithmetic before you buy. Sometimes these sales mean real savings for you, sometimes not. The only way you can tell is by doing your addition and division.

For example, three large cans of name-brand orange juice for a dollar may be labeled "SPECIAL!" by the store. But you aren't saving anything if you can regularly buy the brand in six small cans, equaling the same total number of ounces, for 99 cents.

By the same token, compare the prices in those special displays near the checkout counter with the prices of competitive brands stacked in the regular place in the aisles. Are the displays giving special prices? Usually they are not. They are only arranged there for impulse sales as you get ready to go out and are wondering if you've bought everything you need.

Family excursions to the supermarket can be fun, but they are always expensive. When everybody goes, everybody buys—and those aisles are piled with tempting goodies that your loved ones will drop into your shopping cart. You may as well know how the store managers understand your family's weaknesses:

Your husband finds it hard to resist such treats as hard salami, a beer pack, pretzels, cheeses, antipasto, special crackers and other such exotic items. The store managers will have them out for him.

The children will beg for soft drinks, fancy crackers, chocolate bars and popcorn. These will be shelved so they are within reach of even your toddlers. You'll save money if you let the family sit in the car.

While on the subject of impulse buying, run a check on your own purchase habits. Next time you unpack shopping purchases, set aside all the items you didn't truly have to have—those printed cocktail napkins, for instance, the fancy matches, olives, the new cake mix, salted nuts, the new frozen cheese soufflé. Then total up the prices stamped on them. Was there something else more important that you wanted but felt you couldn't afford?

Save at the produce department

The fancy packages of hand-selected produce are the most expensive, of course, but it pays to compare the prices between the loose untrimmed vegetables and the prepacked ones. Remember that when producers prepackage, they can effect certain mass economies. For example, when useless leaves are trimmed, transportation costs are lower because the vegetables weigh less and take up less space. Sometimes these savings are passed along to you.

Learn how to judge a vegetable's freshness and you'll get more flavor, more vitamins and more eating. Here are the signs to look for:

Artichokes—dark green petals that lie close together.

Asparagus—compact tips, crisp stalks.

Beans (green and wax)—slender, crisp.

Beets—unblemished green leaves (and these are delicious when washed and cooked like spinach).

Broccoli—florets small and green, stalks tender.

Brussels sprouts—dark green and tightly clustered.

Cabbage—compact, leaves crisp.

Cauliflower—head compact, white, unblemished.

Celery—stalks crisp, leaves green.

Corn—kernels fat with milk. (Refrigerate corn instantly when you get it home and husk it just before it goes into boiling unsalted water; salt toughens corn.)

Eggplant—shiny, no rough areas or "rust" spots, heavy for its size.

Lettuce—compact, with crisp leaves.

Limas—pods full and green.

Mushrooms—creamy or ivory-colored, and firm.

Okra pods—crisp and tender.

Onions—skin brittle and hard to the touch.

Parsnips—small, smooth, firm.

Peas—pods full, smooth and bright green. (Peas deteriorate rapidly; cook them in their shells to enhance both tenderness and flavor.)

Potatoes—firm to the touch, no sprouts.

Spinach—small dark leaves.

Squash (acorn and butternut)—firm, green-ridged.

Hubbard variety—hard, with "warts."

Summer squash—yellow, tender, with "warts."

Tomatoes—smooth, firm, no blemishes.

Turnips—heavy, firm.

Zucchini—small- or medium-sized.

Vegetables like asparagus, broccoli, cauliflower and celery are good buys because they do not run largely to inedible leaves, stalks and cores.

Why not try home-canning and freezing of vegetables and fruits when they are abundant and inexpensive? You can find simple directions in any practical cookbook, or write to the U.S. Department of Agriculture, Office of Information, Division of Publications, Washington, D.C.

Canned and packaged savings

Out-of-season vegetables and fruits in cans are especially good values. And they are tasty. They are picked for canning at the peak of their growth—before any deterioration in flavor or nutritional value can take place. To buy them most thriftily, remember this:

In canning, the labor costs for harvesting, preparing, packing, shipping and selling are almost the same, whatever the amount of the contents. You save when you buy in the larger sizes. (But never neglect to check the cost. Every so often it happens that it works out differently on an ounce-by-ounce price.)

In packaged items, too, the large sizes are usually the most economical. The cereal in the small individual packs may cost four cents an ounce, while the king-sized pack of the same cereal comes to only two cents an ounce.

Buy the quality that fits the way you plan to use the food. Why pay for top-grade canned tomatoes when you plan to use them in a stew? A can of "A" tomatoes may cost ten cents more than the same brand and can size marked "B" or "C." The contents of cans "B" and "C" are less uniform and less perfect in shape, but there is no difference in the freshness, in the time they were picked, in their canning process or their nutriment value.

Browse around among the cans of the same brand and size to find any with lower costs that are left over after prices have gone up—you'll often find a few. You pocket the difference.

The private store brands of canned and packaged items almost always cost less than nationally advertised brands. They are usually your best buy. More often than not, they are identical with the nationally advertised brand. As a matter of fact, they often have been bought in bulk from some national canner.

On some foods, however, there may be subtle taste or quality differences and your family will prefer the nationally advertised brand. Sometimes the store brands come in several qualities. Make sure you try the best quality of the store brand before you go back to the national label.

Save on breads

Store brands of bread often cost from 12 to 18 percent less than the well-known advertised breads. Why not try them?

If you're dieting, remember: the least expensive white sliced breads contain the least amount of sugar and, therefore, fewer calories per ounce. You stretch dollars while you shrink your girth.

Head for the second-day bread counter before you browse in the regular bread aisles. Many supermarkets regularly mark down second-day breads, rolls and cakes to half price or less, and today spoilage is rare. Besides, you can put breads and cakes in your refrigerator, when you get home, to maintain freshness for days. There's no reason why you can't even freeze them.

Save dairy dollars

How much money do you spend needlessly for dairy items because you don't know the facts of dairy nutrition? Do you feel guilty when you don't buy butter? Doctors agree that the less expensive margarines made of poly-unsaturated fats are often better, from a health standpoint, in the American diet.

You may also be paying more for margarine than you need to. There is a price spread of 15 cents among the "regular" margarine brands. The "luxury" types cost still more.

What do you get for the difference? Very little. All margarines must comply with government regulations on contents. Compare the listing of ingredients before you give away your money.

The market basket of the shopper who says, "I buy the best for my family," almost certainly will contain a carton of Jumbo white eggs, graded AA or A. But Jumbo eggs, generally weighing more, are not a good buy if they give members of your family more egg than they want or need.

Brown eggs are often cheaper than white ones and have the same nutritional value. There is little difference, if any, in flavor.

Grade B and C eggs are identical in food value with the more expensive AA and A grades. They may (or may not) be slightly less delicate in flavor and their yolks and shells may break more easily. Always use them for cooking.

Grade AA and A eggs are recommended for poaching, coddling, baking, boiling or frying. When they are fresh and have been kept under refrigeration, they have a firmer consistency than B or C eggs.

Never buy eggs that are not kept in refrigerated cases. A nonrefrigerated egg loses as much freshness in a single

week as a refrigerated one does in a month! You get the fresh-
est eggs from a poultry farm or the dealer who gets farm
deliveries every one or two days.

How to judge freshness: since an eggshell is porous
and allows for evaporation, the fresher the egg, the heavier
it will be.

Save at the meat counter

Meat, poultry and fish take from a quarter to a third of
the food budget, so you want the most economical and appetizing ways of bringing them to your table.

Remember that all meats are cheapest in their season.
Plan menus around them when they are plentiful. Bear in
mind that the *cost per eating portion,* rather than the cost
per pound, is what counts.

Does the supermarket really give you a better buy than
the independent store?

There is no question that the independent "prestige"
butchers have better-looking meat. Their merchandise may
also have less waste. An independent butcher is less likely
to sell chickens or chicken parts in which much of the weight
is in the frame. You get less waste in freshly ground hamburger from the independent butcher rather than from the
supermarket's preground, prepackaged type.

But there is no question either that the supermarkets
and chain stores generally have lower prices. The enormous
quantities they buy give them bargaining power; also, since
they are so much interested in price, they pay as little as
possible for butchering.

Some housewives have unreasonable prejudices and
fears about supermarket meat. One housewife who found
the edges of a precut, packaged steak dark and "unappetiz-
ing" decided to switch to a neighborhood butcher. She should
have returned to the chain store at the end of the day—when
meats that show changes in appearance are marked down—
and laid in as many of those steaks as her freezer would hold.
Meat that has turned dark because of too tight packaging

returns to its natural color when unwrapped and exposed to the air.

When you buy supermarket meats, it pays to check the whole meat section before you make your choice. The meat manager spreads his best buys throughout the counter. It also pays to check the whole display carefully because the store may not advertise an especially good buy one week if it happened to advertise the same meat the week before—even though the new price is lower. Also, some wonderful prices never get advertised because the store got a good buy *after* its ad went to press.

Many people think the meat specials are for the weekend only. But some supermarkets offer lower prices in midweek to spread traffic more evenly. It can pay to shop early in the week. Know your store's policies.

Some meat experts say you save more in using your freezer if you buy meats when the cut is best for you (say there is less fat or the sizes are just right) rather than when they are on sale. They say that sales come often enough to meet your needs during the year, but you frequently spend more than you should to get a meat you want for company, for example. If you had picked up one ahead of time, when you came across it at a good price, and frozen it, you would have saved money on company splurges. It's a point to consider.

The expensive cuts of meat we have gotten used to are almost always simpler to prepare than the economical cuts, but no better in terms of nourishment. Often the economical cuts are more flavorful.

Flank steak, elegantly known as London Broil in hotels and restaurants, is not the most economical cut of beef, but it is about 30 cents a pound cheaper than sirloin or porterhouse—and without a bone.

Chuck beef often goes on sale. Buy as much as your freezer will hold. Use it for a savory meat loaf, a beef pie, meatballs and spaghetti or a weekend barbecue. Or prepare it in a stew and package both the meat and the sauce in freezer containers that hold enough for a family meal. Don't add potatoes and vegetables until you heat the stew for dinner.

Fresh brisket of beef is one of the least expensive cuts and ideal for boiled beef. Americans in England order it again and again but seldom eat it at home. Why not?

You don't need an elegant crown roast to enjoy pork. A loin of pork costs less than what the chops it contains would add up to separately, and it makes a delicious dinner.

Buy a shoulder of pork and have it boned and ground for meatballs.

Pork cutlets—actually these are thick slices of a fresh ham—are a good buy because there is no waste.

Bacon is delicious but it offers little nutritional value, and it's expensive. When you want to stretch dollars, don't serve bacon every day with eggs. Keep it for a weekend treat.

A lamb shoulder is relatively inexpensive and makes a fine pot roast. So does a breast, boned and rolled.

Lamb shanks—each gives an individual serving that is sweet and tender when braised or roasted—cost far less than a leg of lamb.

Leftover lamb, minced, makes a fine shepherd's pie with a potato crust.

Buy a leg of lamb when it is on sale and have steaks cut from it to freeze at home.

Veal steaks and cutlets are expensive when bought separately but not when they are cut from a leg of veal that you buy for a roast.

A rump or shoulder of veal, much cheaper than a leg, can be boned and rolled for roasting or pot-roasting. Ask the butcher to do it for you. Ask him for other thrifty tips. He'll give them to you.

For top nutrition at low cost, learn to use the variety meats—liver, kidneys and hearts, for example. The French, admired all over the world for their cooking, make heavy use of these meats.

When it comes to buying poultry, any woman who has a freezer is being extravagant anytime she does not buy a heavy bird, especially the larger turkeys. Large turkeys are cheaper per pound and offer you more meat in proportion to the frame. Half or more of any bird can be frozen. Anytime you see half of a large turkey offered, remember that it may be a more profitable buy than a whole turkey of the same weight.

When you see chicken "on sale," check to see how much weight there is in the frame before you decide that it is a good buy.

Fish, like meat and poultry, is cheapest at the height of its season, and the fresher it is, the more nutritious and flavorful. Some chain stores and supermarkets make an all-out effort to offer fresh fish.

Use natural tenderizers

When a less expensive meat cut would profit from tenderizing, you don't have to buy a commercial tenderizer. Marinate in vinegar, lemon juice, tomatoes or wine from your pantry shelf. These natural tenderizers also lend flavor.

Always remove meat—of any kind or cut—from the refrigerator some time before cooking. Roasts should be given 3 to 4 hours to reach room temperature. Steaks or chops need 1 to 2 hours. Chopped meat, chicken and fish need 1 hour.

Freezing Timetable (at 0°F.)
- Beef, lamb, veal will keep .... up to 1 year
- Chopped meat will keep .... 2 months
- Ham will keep .... 1 month
- Pork will keep .... 4 to 6 months
- Frankfurters will keep .... 1 month
- Poultry will keep .... 4 to 6 months
- Fish will keep .... 4 to 6 months

Leftovers make thrifty meals

Never leave food in the refrigerator until it gets un-
appetizing. With a little imagination you can prepare any
food temptingly. It was the thrift of European housewives,
seeking to use all the odds and ends of food they had ac-
cumulated, that brought about canapés and hors d'oeuvres.
These appetizing tidbits—*hors d'oeuvres* in France, *antipasto* in Italy, *smorgasbord* in Scandinavia and *zakuski* in
Russia—clearly demonstrate that thrift can create a great
cuisine.

To start you off: make a platter of canapés and hors
d'oeuvres out of bits of cheese, tuna fish, salami, frankfurters, chicken, sausage, pickles, olives, hamburger, egg,
celery, ham, beets and onion. Serve them as a complete lunch
or supper, or to go with a soup for dinner.

If there aren't enough leftovers for an hors d'oeuvres
platter, add what you have to the soup itself. Ham or franks
will enrich black bean or lentil soup. Add meatballs to a
consommé or to a beef-and-vegetable soup. Drop some diced
chicken into cream of chicken, sliced carrots into cream of
celery or mushroom soup. Serve the soup with bread or rolls
that are no longer on the fresh side, toasted with herbed or
garlic butter or margarine.

Do it yourself and save

The more labor you buy toward the preparation of any
packaged or frozen food, the higher the price. For instance:

Six fresh potatoes for baking cost about 72 cents in one
area, for example. But you pay $1.14 for 6 frozen baked
potatoes with a negligible cheese topping.

Grated cheese in shaker tops costs about 50 percent
more than when you grate it yourself.

TV dinners often don't satisfy and the taste of some
leaves much to be desired. A frozen packaged dinner can
cost two and three times as much as the same food in the
same quantity when prepared at home. Use only such meals
when you need the convenience.

The peas and lima beans that come shelled in little baskets always cost more. Always, too, they should be examined for freshness. Dealers sometimes shell these vegetables when their pods proclaim advancing age.

Save while cooking

Your cooking techniques and repertoire can stretch your food dollar.

When you roast meats, for example, you lose some from shrinkage. The higher the oven temperature, the more shrinkage. But many housewives still roast at top temperatures. Use a cookbook that tells you how to prepare meats using no more than 300 degrees F., and you'll save a surprising amount of food. Your roasts will also be more flavorful and more tender.

Low cooking temperatures also mean less crumbling—which gives you more good slices—when you carve. You'll save on fuel costs. You need to do less basting and, later, less cleanup from spatter.

Learn to use stuffings and gravies as meat extenders and for variety when you emphasize low-cost meats.

And build a good repertoire of dishes that use ground meats, which are the least expensive to buy and have no waste. Use ground beef, lamb and pork for variety in these dishes. They can be broiled or served in meat pies, casseroles and meat loaves.

Keep alert

The Commissioners of Markets all over the country urge shoppers to keep alert when they are buying in order to make money-saving discoveries. You will learn that:

The size of a can or package can be deceptive, but the weight marked on it will be accurate.

Similar, even identical, items cost less under different names. A can of "mixed fruit," for instance, costs less than a can of "fruit salad" or "fruit for salad."

In a can or a package labeled "Spaghetti and Meat-

balls" the emphasis will be on the spaghetti. There only have
to be two meatballs to live up to the label. There may indeed
be two only, and they may be small. On the other hand, in a
can or package labeled "Meatballs and Spaghetti" the emphasis will be on the meatballs. Similarly, the package or
can labeled "Shrimp and Rice" will contain more shrimp
than the one labeled "Rice and Shrimp."

Never forget that in spite of regular government inspection there are still fraudulent scales at work. Or, while
a customer's eyes focus on the weight indicator, a scale may
get surreptitious pressure from a storekeeper's thumb or
elbow.

Before you buy, make sure that the sides of the little
cardboard or plastic boxes in which berries and shelled vegetables, shallots, plum tomatoes and such are sold have not
been bent in—"starfished"—so they hold less.

The trouble you take clipping coupons from newspapers
and magazines to get five or ten cents off a purchase price
may save you nothing. Some storekeepers feel that the re-
demption of such coupons is a nuisance, and increase their
prices accordingly. To promote a larger order, a salesman
tells the store manager in advance that the coupon is about
to appear. The manager can simply stamp the new order with
a higher price. Does this kind of thing happen at your "favorite" store?

It also pays to keep an eye on the checkout clerks. Their
errors, careless rather than deliberate since they gain nothing from them, can cost you money. One woman who recently took the time and trouble to check her $33.92 order, as
she unpacked it at home, found that she was overcharged
by $2.58.

Remember that when any store "gives" you anything,
you have to pay for it one way or another. Some stores discount all sales slips by 10 percent at a certain time, usually
a midweek morning between nine and 12. No store, of course,
can afford to give away such a discount unless its normal
prices are high enough to make up for this. Also, you will

usually discover that neither the shelves nor the refrigerated cases are stocked for a discount day. You'll have to return to buy whatever else is needed at the higher price.

POINTS TO REMEMBER

1. Your biggest dollar-saver is planning and comparison-shopping. Know all the supermarkets in your area. Store brands are usually the least expensive and just as good as the nationally advertised brands.

2. Read your daily newspaper for advertised specials; plan your menus by the week around these specials.

3. Buy your vegetables—from artichokes to zucchini—at their cheapest, and best, seasons.

4. If you know enough about nutrition, you can make substitutions on canned goods, dairy products and at the meat counter—for less money but with the same food value.

5. Your cooking techniques (the right heat, for example) can stretch your food dollar. Also, collect recipes that will help turn your leftovers into tasty meals.

Chapter Three

YOUR CLOTHING DOLLAR

Not where you shop or what you pay but *what you buy* makes the difference between a smart wardrobe and a dowdy one. A smart wardrobe can be low cost. The dowdy one can be expensive at any price. The more advantageously you stretch your clothing dollar, the larger and more enjoyable your wardrobe can be.

We are told that the "average" American family spends about 10 percent of its income on clothing. Are you spending more or less than this average? Can you do better?

Both men and women can save clothing dollars and have a more useful wardrobe by planning closely around their specific individual activities. Buy sparingly, but custom-build a wardrobe around daily work and other pursuits as carefully as around your body build.

A homemaker, for instance, can save money and be more comfortable working in jeans or shorts and a bright blouse around the house, when marketing or doing other such chores. Or she can stick to the simplest cotton dresses, saving her money for dress-up and sports clothes. An outdoors worker does not require as many suits as an office worker, but he needs lots of sturdy, machine-washable items.

Whenever you go out to buy, decide clearly first *what* you need, for *what* specific purposes. Refuse to be turned from your goal.

Once you find a store that sells clothing you like at the

price range you can afford, save money by having a favorite salesperson call you to tell you of the good values and to hold them aside for you. Learn the store's sale times and be on hand to get its best buys.

It always pays to keep shopping elsewhere, too. Make sure other new retailers aren't offering more for your money.

Consider maintenance costs

Your clothing dollar has to include maintenance as well as original cost. A man's wash-and-wear shirt may cost $5 compared with $3.50 for a similar cotton. But if you have to spend 25 cents to send the cotton out to the laundry, the "less expensive" shirt will have cost you $5 anyway by the sixth laundering. After that, the wash-and-wear done at home begins saving you money. You also save the bother and cost of cracked buttons, rips and weakened fabrics caused by rough outside handling and harsh chemicals.

A woman's ten-dollar skirt in a fabric that must be dry-cleaned and pressed professionally will soon eat up a lot more dollars than a 12-dollar skirt that can be washed and ironed lightly at home.

Learn label language

Read the labels carefully before you decide to buy. Here are the most common terms used in labels, and what they mean:

Colorfast. To what extent does it exist? Sometimes this term is used loosely. Not all "colorfast" fabrics resist sun, water and perspiration. The more *generally resistant* a fabric is, the more *specific* its label is likely to be.

Drip-dry. Such clothing should be hung up when wet. Don't dry or wring it. Let the water, dripping down and off, smooth the wrinkles.

Permanent-press. These fabrics were introduced for moderately priced fan-pleated skirts, and later in men's wear. They are exactly as named—permanently pressed. Permanent pleats can make alterations difficult; hemlines, even on unpleated skirts, can often be shortened but not lengthened. The finish is built in by an addition to the fabric and is not affected by washing.

Preshrunk. These fabrics may shrink from 3 percent to 5 percent. When they are labeled *Sanforized,* they shrink only about half as much. Knitted fabrics may shrink up to 10 percent. Preshrunk fabrics can take long, hard wear.

Spot-repellent. These fabrics have been surface-treated so that anything spilled will not impregnate the weave and can easily be wiped off.

Wash-and-wear. A resin finish usually contributes this quality. The item may require some ironing even when new, and almost certainly will need ironing after many launderings.

Wrinkle-resistant. This is protected with a resin finish, which also means less shrinkage and some protection from spotting.

A note about imports. Check the fit and workmanship yourself, as imports are not always carefully checked during manufacture. Imports offer exclusivity, but the costs of freight and duty have been going up and may offset any advantage in the rate of exchange with the country from which they come.

Understand the new fibers

New fiber names are appearing on labels so frequently that you may be tempted to think they are more or less alike. But a new name may herald a new development and usually offers something extra. Here are the various specialized fibers, their uses and their "trade" names as now commonly seen.

Acetate and triacetate. Used in knitted fabrics for men's sports clothes and children's items. Has some resistance to wrinkles. Should be dry-cleaned unless label states otherwise. If laundered, press with warm iron only. Trade names: Acele, Arnel, Avicolor, Avisco Acetate, Celanese, Celaperm, Chromspun, Colorsealed, Estron.

Acrylic. Found in knit and woven fabrics. Wrinkle-resistant, gives warmth. Check label to see whether dry-cleaning or laundering is recommended. Use warm iron only. Known as Acrilan, Creslan, Orlon, Zefron.

Nylon. Largely colorfast and wrinkle-resistant. Washes easily, dries rapidly, requires little ironing. Excellent in lingerie, knitted fabrics, hosiery. Called Agilon, Ban-Lon, Chemstrand, Nylex.

Polyester. Often combined with cotton in men's shirts, women's and children's apparel. Used extensively in knitted goods. Wrinkle-resistant, also sun-, moth- and mildew-resistant. Does not shrink, dries quickly, needs only touch-up ironing under low heat. Often called Avilan, Dacron, Fortrel, Kodel, Terylene, Vycron.

Rayon. Inexpensive, combines well with all fibers. When combined with polyester, holds press. Used in many different textures. Follow manufacturer's instructions for dry-cleaning or laundering. Labeled: Avisco, Avril, Avron, Bemberg, Celanese, Coloray, Cupioni, Cupracolor, Enka, Fortisan, Jetspun, Nupron, Zantrel.

Spandex. Has excellent stretch qualities which make it popular in women's foundation garments, bathing suits, support hose, snow suits and ski pants. Should not be exposed to high heat. Machine-wash and dry at low temperature. Do not iron. Look for it as: Duraspan, Glospan, Lycra, Spandelle, Stretch-Ever, Vyrene.

Use natural fibers correctly

The natural fibers offer special advantages, but you need to know how they are best used:

Cotton, when crushproof, is durable. Preshrunk, it washes and irons easily.

Imported cotton is not always preshrunk and costs three or four times more than domestic cottons.

Linen, more expensive than cotton, wrinkles and creases but when freshly laundered has a charmingly cool look. It washes like a handkerchief.

Silk, essentially a luxury fabric, is usually expensive. Cheaper silks have often been weighted and may not be lasting.

Wool, with its great warmth, may be virgin wool or used wool that has been reprocessed. Its label will state which, and will also tell the proportionate addition of any other fabric. Wool should be preshrunk.

Weaves, too, have an effect on wear. For example:

Tweed, even when loosely woven, will wear indefinitely.

Velour, with a pile that will hold up for a long time, is practical and durable.

Velvet and velveteen, made of silk nylon or rayon, should not be expected to give long or hard wear. Stains and perspiration, likely to mat the fabric, tend to be permanent. *Velveteen* is sturdy when cotton-backed. *Velveteen corduroy* is also sturdy.

Wool jersey, which is not woven but knitted, is an excellent buy. It comes in varying weights, suitable to many purposes.

How to check for quality

You can't expect high-quality workmanship in low-cost men's clothes or, for example, in a woman's dress that sells for $15 or less at its regular price. Beyond that, remember that quality workmanship means the garment will look better and wear better. In moderate and high-priced clothes, check to see that:

A pattern is matched well at seams, armholes and collar.

Buttonholes have reinforced ends and the buttons fit the buttonholes.

Heavy-wear clothing has extra stitching and is reinforced at points of wear.

Seams are at least ½ inch wide and pinked or finished against raveling.

Side openings lie flat when closed.

Hem is 3 inches deep and, if the material tends to ravel, taped.

Any lining is wide and long enough.

Stitches are small and do not pull.

Both the lining and padding of washable clothes will take soap and water.

Give clothing day-by-day care

Whatever you pay for them, clothes look better and last longer when you give them proper care. Air them after each wearing. Arrange them on hangers carefully, with the collar or neckline and shoulder seams straight and with the trousers or skirt hanging free and uncrowded. Dry-clean or launder clothing before dirt and stains become ingrained. Spot-clean whenever necessary to cut down on the wear and cost of frequent dry-cleaning or laundering.

How to save at clothing sales

The regular clothing sales offer undoubted bargains. They are normally scheduled at specific times. They are held in luxury specialty shops, department stores, discount houses and bargain basements.

At any sale, the early bird catches the best buys. The longer a sale goes on, in hours or days, the less choice remains. If you plan your purchases well ahead, you can build up a complete wardrobe, all at sale prices.

The greater the markdown, the more closely you should examine the item for tears or for defects of workmanship or fit that may make it useless to you. Usually you can't return sale merchandise.

Unless it fits a true need, don't buy—because is isn't a savings at any price, but an indulgence.

If you don't like it as much as you would at full price, don't buy, because you won't wear it but only let it hang in your closet.

Watch out for "50 percent off" sales. If the store holding a 50 percent off sale is not well established and known to you, you may be better off avoiding it: 50 percent off what? Irresponsible merchants have been known to raise their prices more than 50 percent—just before these sales.

Go early to the "come-on" sale

When the hard-to-believe advertisement reads "Men's National Brand Topcoats at $18.39," or "Mink Capes at $100," it's often a "come-on." More often than not, the number of topcoats or mink capes—or anything else so advertised —will be limited. To benefit from such a sale you have to be at the store when the doors open and make your way, without delay, to the advertised merchandise, or there will be none left when you arrive.

Here are the regular clothing sales held by reputable stores:

Reduced for Clearance sales offer the best buys in men's, women's and children's clothes. The savings often are 50 percent, sometimes as much as 75 percent.

However, a store may bring in additional merchandise on which the manufacturers and the store have taken a low markup to make these sales more attractive. Rarely, if ever, are the added items as good a bargain as those really marked down for clearance. Generally the items from the store's regular stock have the original price crossed out on the tags. But judge the quality for yourself, too.

Pre-Clearance sales are less dramatic bargains, but bargains nevertheless. The choice is wider than you will find later at the clearance.

Special Purchase sales generally offer items on which both a manufacturer and the store have cut their normal markup to make the sale possible. These sales do not, as a rule, give you savings of more than 10 to 20 percent.

National Brand Men's Clothes which go on sale semi-annually represent savings of about 10 percent. But 10 percent saved is 10 percent earned. And here there can be no question about the values. The times for these sales vary, so watch for them in newspapers.

Men's and Women's Coats and sometimes suits and rainwear go on sale Columbus Day and Election Day. The stores plan these sales months in advance and they offer true bargains.

Shoe sales are held usually in January and July and can get you savings of up to 50 percent on national brands.

Women's Spring Suit and Coat sales take place in May and early June, depending upon locality and, occasionally, on the weather.

Summer Clothes, including sheer dresses, bathing suits, patio coats and beach wraps, go to the marked-down racks in July. Whatever remains will be marked down further at a later date. You'll have less choice, but you might want to chance it.

Lingerie sales take place several times a year and the times vary. But those held from the end of December to the middle of January (when the store is satisfied that most Christmas merchandise that is to be returned has come back) offer the best bargains. They are particularly great when a store buyer was overoptimistic about the Christmas sale volume.

Stocking sales of name brands are held at regular times which vary from store to store. They offer savings of 10 percent. The sales of "irregulars," in which the imperfections are often extremely difficult to discern, have 25 percent lower prices.

Furs traditionally go on sale in January and August, and these sales offer worthwhile savings.

Handbag sales generally are in January and July and offer from moderate to sensational savings. These are often a clearinghouse for various manufacturers as well as for the store that holds the sale.

Tips for saving on men's clothing

The specialty chain stores usually offer the best values in men's clothing. But a man needs good fit in a suit above all else. It pays to shop the place that provides a topnotch fitter. Avoid a "bargain" if you have to use a neighborhood tailor for even minor alterations. The neighborhood man will charge as much or more than you saved on your "bargain," and if he is not good, the suit, jacket or trousers will never be right. A store fitter has the advantage of knowing the suit's construction. He has altered the same suit for many different builds. And fitting is free at most men's stores.

If possible, squeeze money out of the family budget to give an office-worker husband at least five suits—one for each workday of the week. He can wear a suit for one day only and give it a full week to hang out until the next wearing. Any wrinkles left can be hand-pressed at home. He avoids the cost, trouble and wear of constantly having suits pressed by the dry cleaner. Suits should go out for dry-cleaning no more than once or twice a year—and never, if possible, for pressing.

Buy suits and jackets in colors that go easily with different-colored shirts and pants. One suit, if worn with a blue shirt one day, a yellow shirt at the next wearing, and a striped one the third time, with a change of ties each wearing as well, looks almost like three different kinds of suits.

Good permanent-press slacks are expensive but save money in the long run.

The hard-finish worsteds wear longer and need less cleaning and pressing than flannels and other soft fabrics. But be wary of suits, jackets or pants that show a gloss when new. They will rapidly acquire a "shine" and look worn.

Weatherproofed topcoats with detachable linings are most practical. They are all-weather, often all-year coats.

Be wary when stores claim, "Nationally advertised at ... Our price ..." One man, for example, found a jacket with a tag that said, "Nationally advertised at $55. Our price: $45." Later he saw the same jacket at a more expensive shop for $50. He had saved, but not as much as he thought.

How to buy shirts and accessories

Sales on men's shirts are the retailer's favorite device to bring people into the store. They are so frequent, and so often offer national brands, that it should never be necessary to buy a man's shirt at a regular price.

Shirts are great wardrobe extenders. A man should have not only white but also solid colors, striped and discreetly patterned shirts for variety in his dress. Shirts should be fully cut and carry a preshrunk label that guarantees the entire shirt, not only part of it. These will not shrink more than 2 percent and will wear better and look better.

Wash-and-wear shirts save money in the long run. They can be washed and quickly ironed at home. A combination of 65 percent polyester and 35 percent cotton is generally recommended.

Permanent-press shirts look a little coarser than those of other fabrics, but they come in attractive patterns and colors and save a nice piece of the laundry bill.

Cotton broadcloth that is not wash-and-wear is still a good shirt fabric. It launders well and maintains a good appearance.

Comparatively unknown shirt brands may offer better value than the shirts with labels of well-known manufacturers. They are worth shopping for if you get the same quality for less money.

Neckties also help a man to stretch his wardrobe. They are a personal mood item. No man should be pushed to wear a tie he doesn't like because someone who loves him bought it for him. Better to give him tie money on gift-giving occasions and let him choose his own (at the after-holiday sales). Ties keep their new appearance longer if they are worn no more than once every two weeks and allowed to hang out properly between times.

Men's tie tacks and cuff links are well styled today even in the moderately priced lines. You find the best buys in chain specialty stores and discount houses. Don't buy them just before Easter, Father's Day, Graduation Day or Christmas, when prices tend to be inflated.

Men's socks cost less annually when they are all of the same color—or no more than two colors. New pairs can be matched up when a hole develops and there is less work in finding pairs after laundering.

Save money on hats by simply not wearing any, whenever possible. If you do wear any, keep them in better shape longer by unsnapping the brim when the hat is not in use. Replace sweatband before a hat gets stained.

When a jacket shows worn elbows, apply elbow patches found in notions departments. They are fashionable.

Shirt collars that wear out can be replaced by collars that are sold at the notions counters of department and variety stores. They come in all types and sizes.

To keep men's winter clothing safely through summer, have it rough dry-cleaned (not pressed) in the spring and store it in airtight plastic coverings. Turn out the cuffs and collars on shirts.

Tips for saving on women's clothing

Plan your wardrobe around the classic styles—and you will get more mileage from each item in your closet. The classics and near-classics can span many seasons, while each year's high fashions soon become dated.

Classics also give you better value in fabrics and workmanship. A manufacturer will invest more in the perennial shirtwaist dress, for instance, because he figures that sooner or later these will sell, while the high-fashion novelties that are seen everywhere soon vanish from sight. He has to sell them fast or perhaps sell them off.

Buy versatility

Stretch dollars by concentrating on styles that can be dressed up or down to suit varying occasions. The more limited your wardrobe, the more you need such flexible fashions. It's better to invest a little more in a dress that is many-purposed than to spend less for a dress in a style or color that limits it to a single look.

Separates are savers. Invest in separates. They give the greatest amount of variety and versatility. Choose jackets, blouses, sweaters and skirts that go together in their lines, fabrics and colors. Learn to mix and match them with imagination to give you the frequent lift of wearing something "new" of your own "creation."

Clever accessories such as scarves, ascots, bibs, belts and jewelry can help you turn many new dressing tricks for special occasions from separates already in your closet. They save you the cost of last-minute emergency purchases.

The untrimmed coat is smarter. A winter coat without a fur collar is less expensive to buy than a fur-trimmed one and usually more adaptable. If you want a touch of fur at the neck, why not buy a little fur ascot, boa or collar that can dress up many coats, suits and dresses?

Buy color

Choose colors with special care. Invest time in finding the colors that do the most for you. Avoid those that depress or don't flatter, no matter how great a "bargain" the garment might be. The red dress that washes out a woman's color, the green T-shirt that does nothing for a child, are no bargain at any price. But watch out for preconceived ideas. Sometimes the particular shade of a color makes a big difference.

When you are dollar-stretching, don't buy a dress, suit or coat in a color that forces you to buy a special pair of shoes or a bag, a hat or gloves to go with it. Make sure the color goes with accessories you already have.

Buy good fit

Proper fit is one of the most important elements in buying dresses, suits and coats. When they fit your figure, they look better, please you more and wear longer, no matter how inexpensive they were to begin with.

Never spend so much for a dress, suit or coat that you have nothing left over for the alterations you may need. These can be expensive. Fitting yourself is not easy, but you can have a garment "pin-fitted" by the store fitter, which costs little and sometimes nothing, and carry on from there yourself. Usually you can also find a neighborhood dressmaker who will charge less than the store's alteration department.

Where to shop

The styling of merchandise in women's specialty chain stores has been getting better and they now offer very good values in coats, suits, dresses, shoes, hats, lingerie, blouses, scarves, stockings. In some neighborhood specialty shops, a dress may cost from one to three dollars less than the same model by the same manufacturer in a department store.

But, in general, department store regular prices are still lower than specialty shop prices. You have a larger variety to choose from, at a wider range of prices, and sales offer more choice.

The bargain basements of department stores offer clothes at much lower prices than upstairs. Their buyers rarely use the same manufacturers shopped by the upstair buyers. The basements have been tending more to self-service, which lowers their overhead and allows still lower prices. Sometimes they buy high-priced closeouts from their own upper floors and from those of big stores all over the country. They sell these at less than half price. They are worth getting to know.

Try the discount houses that offer designer clothes, usually with the labels removed, at low prices. They buy up samples of fashions that were discontinued from a wholesaler's line, and they buy up end lots. Sometimes manufacturers are eager for greater volume and make up more garments for them. You may go to a discount store many times without finding anything right for you. Then during one visit you will find a coat, suit, dress, bathing suit or housecoat that hardly makes a dent in your budget.

Many new small "boutiques" have sprung up in recent years. They are established by young people to carry high-style clothes. Prices in some are high, and in some incredibly low. Often the high-priced garments are offered on sale at considerable savings. If the style suits your taste and life, you can find, at moderate cost, the kind of flair that ordinarily comes only in high-priced designer clothes. These boutiques cut many dollars from your leisure-clothes wardrobe.

The latest in this field are the "discount boutiques." Their regular prices are good and their sales offer clothing at fantastic savings.

Can they get it for you wholesale?

Beware the stores that claim to sell at "wholesale" prices. The real wholesalers are not in the retail business. They are geared to deal with specialty shops, department stores and discount houses that give them large orders. They do not allow individual customers into their showrooms unless they have some special reason for giving someone this unusual privilege.

The business that advertises "wholesale" prices to the public is seeking retail business and is a retailer—and is trying to sell under false colors. The sales tend to be final. You will find it hard and unpleasant, if not impossible, to exchange a purchase, even if you just want another size or color.

Save stocking dollars

Stockings run up to a shockingly high amount of wardrobe dollars. Cut back by not wearing them whenever the weather and situation permit. When you are working at home, for example, try peds or knee or ankle socks. For many women, an attractive leg tan works as dollar-saver for many months of the year—keeps you cooler in hot weather, too.

Stockings with elasticity of weave fit smoothly and wear best. Test the stocking by stretching at the top, the toe and the heel. How far does it stretch? When you release your hold, does it return immediately to its original shape?

Never buy stockings just before Christmas, Easter or Mother's Day—prices always go up.

Plan to stock up at the regular sales held in department and chain stores when even top name-brand stockings go down in price. Buy enough pairs to last you until the next sale.

You stretch stocking dollars when you buy the same

color in large quantities—three, six, even a dozen pairs at a time. As one stocking rips you can make new matching pairs, down to the next-to-the-last stocking. Also, you don't waste your own time matching up pairs after laundering.

Try the new panty-hose stockings in the heavier weaves. They can save stocking money if they give you better fit, with less stocking tension and fewer runs.

Make sure your stocking size and length is right for you. Many women rip stockings more frequently than they should because the sizes they buy are too tight or the proportions (length below and above the knee) are wrong for them. Shop carefully to find the brands that are cut and shaped best for you, rather than for new colors.

Costume jewelry gets expensive

Cleverly chosen costume jewelry adds flair to a simple wardrobe—but it can also be a dollar-waster. Those shiny and colorful bits of glitter can be tempting in their brilliantly lighted cases : be careful. Don't buy costume jewelry for itself alone. The glitter will soon go and you just indulged in an impulsive extravagance. Ask yourself : "What does this piece of jewelry do for my clothes?" You get endless mileage from one well-designed, important gold or silver pin and a good string of pearls and pearl earrings—they need not even be cultured.

Is this fur really necessary?

Before you decide that you must have a fur coat, be sure you really need the warmth. Some women think they must have one to impress their crowd, when actually the others envy their smart use of handsome cloth coats—and their independent spirit. How often will you actually wear a fur coat? For what specific uses?

Consider the stylish new fake and "fun" furs. These are made of synthetics or, if real, generally of rabbit skins. Some are dyed to look like ocelot, zebra and other skins, and some are in bright colors and gay patterns. They give fine warmth. The synthetics need no storage and dry quickly when caught in the rain. They cost around $100 in the big chains.

Women who prefer rabbit skins, because they are actual fur, can find them at prices competitive with the synthetics. But they will molt; they may wear less satisfactorily, since fur gets brittle when it dries out.

Once you are in the market for the more expensive furs, remember that some will take good care *of you*, but others need good care *from* you. The long-haired furs are generally less expensive than the flat furs, give you more warmth and are more durable.

Can you serve your purposes with a coat that isn't full length? It will be less expensive, because fewer pelts and less workmanship are required. You need not worry about hemlines that go up and down each season. It will be lighter on your back and less bulky when you ride.

Buy furs at *reliable* stores. Watch for sales in August, January and on Election Day. Stay away from stores that promise to "get it for you wholesale." Some women have found furs at reliable thrift shops at prices so low that they found it economical to have a local furrier alter, repair and restyle them—provided the garments did not require too much work.

Here are the dollar-stretching sturdy furs:

Beaver—very warm but relatively expensive
Fitch—moderately priced, moderate warmth
Krimmer—moderately priced, good warmth
Muskrat—moderately priced, good warmth
Mouton—one of the least expensive furs, good warmth
Nutria—moderately priced, good warmth
Persian lamb—expensive, good warmth
Sheared raccoon—moderately priced, good warmth

Try home sewing

A woman who makes most of her own clothes and sews

for her children claims that her electric sewing machine "does everything but sing 'God Save the Queen!'" The new machines can do so many kinds of stitches that in very little time you save enough money to cover the cost of a good one, a course in dressmaking, and sewing equipment, including an inflatable dress form that helps you do a better job more easily.

Millions of women are sewing at home now for good reasons. Today's styles are simple, and quality ready-made clothes cost so much.

Children's clothes usually don't even have a waistline and don't need much tailoring skill. You can easily do better than the expensive ready-mades that often are neither color-fast nor durable, have poor construction, skimpy seams and badly cut armholes.

Learn to make your own "best" dresses, suits and skirts. Use the luxury fabrics and the dressmaking details that are so expensive when you buy ready-mades. You don't save much by making yourself everyday dresses in inexpensive fabrics. The makers of budget and moderate-priced clothes do such a high-volume business that they can buy fabrics at little more than cost, and they have little labor in mass cuttings. But such clothes are so simple, you may find making them worthwhile anyway.

Don't "splurge" on children's clothes

Fancy clothing of careful workmanship for babies and young children may flatter a parent's ego—but they are expensive and they don't have any meaning for children. They are quickly outgrown. Don't pay for the long wear that comes from careful workmanship unless there are younger sisters and brothers who will soon inherit the items. Remember that fashions can make children's clothing obsolete, too. The younger ones may not have the same build as the older child, either.

Children are comfortable and happy in simple T-shirts and polo shirts, slacks, shorts, sweaters, jumpers and jeans.

These are also the least expensive children's clothes. Make sure they are washable in automatic machines and can go through your dryer without shrinking.

Children do need to feel proud of their looks. Select with an eye to their builds and preferences. A turtleneck, for example, does nothing for a boy or girl with a round baby face.

Take youngsters shopping with you. When they help you to buy, you will be stretching your dollar. Children begin to be aware of their looks long before they can put their feelings into words. They often let good clothes remain unused in closets and drawers until outgrown because they don't really like the way they look in them.

Chain specialty stores and national mail order stores offer especially good value in children's clothing and are up-to-the-minute in children's fashions. A little comparative shopping will tell you which local stores carry fashions that are best for you.

Great dollar-savers—especially when children are small and growing fast—are the "children's exchanges." These are small stores that take good, slightly used, outgrown clothing (and sports equipment) and resell them—often at far less than half the original price. These clothes are always cleaned and in excellent condition. You can even resell them to the store if they are still good when your child outgrows them.

A neighborhood sports shop sometimes runs a children's exchange for sports equipment. One such store, for example, exchanges ice skates for $1.50 plus an outgrown pair of skates. Another store exchanges ski equipment. Such sensible shops are run as private businesses, by good-cause organizations, and in some private schools. They can cut your expenses for children's items down to an incredible low. The makes of their merchandise are generally expensive, too.

Doctors tell us that children don't need expensive shoes, but they do need well-fitting ones. Buy the cheapest brands as long as the store does a careful fitting job, allowing plenty of room for growth. Never keep a child in shoes that begin to hamper growth, or you can cause real health problems. Sometimes children need new shoes every three months. Not all chain store shoes wear as well as the standard brands, but some wear better. In any event, they usually are durable enough to last until they are outgrown.

POINTS TO REMEMBER

1. Buy only what you really need for your specific work and your other activities. Study labels carefully in terms of wearability, cleaning requirements and other information. Give clothes proper day-by-day care to make them last longer.

2. Search for the retailers who offer the best values. Plan your needs in advance so you can buy all, or almost all, of your wardrobe at the various seasonal sales.

3. Fit is as important as fashion and color. Men should shop at stores with good alteration services, invest in articles that cut laundering and pressing costs.

4. Women should have dresses and suits store-pinned but altered elsewhere, and build their wardrobes around classic fashions. Separates and accessories are good wardrobe extenders.

5. Never splurge on children's clothes since they prefer casual dress and soon outgrow everything anyway.

Chapter Four

FURNISHING
A HOME

The biggest dollar savers when you furnish a home are imagination—and the willingness to do-it-yourself. Imagination can show you how to use hand-me-down and second-hand things in new ways. It not only saves you money but also gives a distinctive touch to your home.

The tall wardrobes our grandparents used in their closetless homes make handsome and stylish armoires for a bar, for books or hi-fi equipment. You can install a few shelves and replace the wood panels in the doors with chicken wire or grillwork to lighten the overall effect.

An old Victorian chair can get a "face-lifting" by being upholstered in a bright chintz or houndstooth check. You can get reupholstering expertise in booklets sold in home-sewing and notions stores.

Cut off the legs of a dreary old chifforobe—and you have a handsome buffet or storage chest. You can strip the old finish, using solvents sold in paint stores.

An old ironwork gate, mounted on legs, can be turned into a coffee table. If you're afraid that food will fall through the grill, top it with a piece of plain glass, half an inch thick.

Unfinished furniture is inexpensive, easy to paint or stain and practical—especially for a playroom or children's room. If you buy it unassembled be sure you get good instructions. Check all the pieces to make sure none are warped.

Go to auctions. You can get rugs, hangings, lighting

fixtures, fireplaces, paneling, even doors for very little money when old mansions and hotels are being demolished.

When you buy furniture, carpeting and appliances in the regular retail stores, remember this: the money involved when you decide that you dislike a particular tie after a few wearings won't upset long-range plans. When you buy expensive items like furniture, carpeting and appliances, you can't afford any mistakes.

Analyze your tastes. Before shopping for furniture, decide which styles or periods you and your family prefer. A low-priced Chippendale reproduction may seem like a great buy now. But will you still think of it as a bargain if your spouse spends the next ten years grumbling that he really wanted something modern? Make sure you are buying styles you can live with for many years, rather than the ones being promoted right now.

Become a questioning shopper. Get down on your hands and knees to examine the density of a carpet's pile. Pull drawers out of bureaus to see how the corners are joined. Lie down on the mattress right in the store. See if the dealer will arrange a demonstration of a washer or dryer. Ask plenty of questions. If two salesmen offer vastly different descriptions of the same item, it means you need a third opinion. Read the brochures put out by manufacturers that tell you how to judge quality.

Plan your color scheme in advance. When you buy carpeting and upholstered furniture, take along something that shows the colors you have in your home now. Don't trust to memory; what looks like a pure red in the store may seem surprisingly orange or pink next to the fabrics you already have. Many stores will give you a small sample so you can judge the color in your home light.

Buy when you can afford to pay cash. Eighty-five percent of carpeting, furniture and appliances are bought on the installment plan. Yet these items are cheaper by about 18 percent—the cost of the carrying charges—when they are bought for cash. That's almost one-fifth the total cost.

Wait for the sales. Many department stores offer sale prices regularly twice a year, August and January or February as a rule. You can get anywhere from 10 percent to 50 percent off the regular prices. The most spectacular markdowns are on floor samples throughout the year, offered because the manufacturer has changed designs. If you know quality, and the usual cost of a manufacturer's line, you can sometimes take home fine furniture for almost a song. But always examine it closely for wear and tear.

Specialty furniture stores outside city limits usually sell at 15 percent less than the department store's regular prices.

The clearance centers maintained by many large stores in the suburbs can be a gold mine, if you're careful and have an open mind. These centers serve as outlets for the big stores' line ends, for the discontinued items and "as is" or shopworn merchandise. The savings are usually phenomenal. You may have to go back several times to find what you want. "As is" merchandise must be inspected carefully on the spot as most clearance centers do not allow returns or exchanges.

Discount houses offer substantial savings, but you may have to foot the bill for delivery yourself. In recent years more manufacturers of nationally advertised furniture have started selling to discount houses, so they can give you a better selection than formerly.

Shop in reliable stores and be wary of advertisements that offer three rooms of furniture at a ridiculously low price, for you're bound to get inferior merchandise. No matter where you buy, find out whether there are hidden costs for warehousing and delivery so you can make true price comparisons.

Save on floor coverings

It's not always necessary to invest in carpets and rugs. A bare wood floor may be just as attractive and easy to maintain as a carpet. Or see if you can cover the floor with the new vinyls and other smooth surface floor coverings that are used today for the whole house. Don't be impressed by maga-

zine pictures of kitchen rugs and wall-to-wall bathroom carpeting—they are impractical.

Whether you buy seconds of tiles for 15 cents apiece to
install yourself, or expensive carpeting, you should have a
good idea of just how much you'll need before you go out to
comparison-shop. To gauge the number of square yards, mul-
tiply the length of the space to be covered by its width, then
divide by nine. If you're buying wall-to-wall carpeting or
sheet vinyl, always insist that the dealer come to your home
and measure himself.

Rug and carpeting know-how

Carpeting comes in three forms: wall-to-wall, large
room-sized rugs and smaller area rugs.

Wall-to-wall carpeting covers the floor completely, giving a feeling of luxury and spaciousness. It's profitable for
the manufacturer because you have to buy much more carpeting to cover the entire floor. The installation, which may
mean considerable cutting and fitting, also costs money.
Cleaning is expensive. Refitting, if you move, means another
large bill for picking up and installing again. Avoid this type.

Rugs, either room-sized or area, don't need installation.
They also can be turned once in a while so that no one part
gets all the wear all the time. Rugs are considered room-sized
when they leave a border of 3 to 12 inches exposed. They are
available in several standard sizes: 8 x 10 feet, 9 x 12 feet,
12 x 15 feet, etc.

Area rugs run smaller: 2 x 5 feet and 4 x 6 feet, for
example, and they come in a wide variety of shapes. A small
vivid accent rug can set off a conversation corner and be all
the carpet you need to furnish a room.

No one factor makes a carpet a "good" or a "bad" buy.
It depends on the thickness of the pile, whether it is tufted,
woven or knitted, the type of fiber, the weight of the yarn,
the strength of the backing and the quality of the underpadding. Not all of this is visible to the unprofessional eye. But
by folding back a corner of the carpeting you can get a pretty

good idea of the density of the pile, the way the fibers are attached and the sturdiness of the backing.

Greater density—when the tufts are close together—gives better wearability as a general rule. The backing holds the carpeting together, prevents stretching, shrinking and buckling, but to accomplish this, it should have a decent coating of latex. The underpadding acts as a shock absorber, extending the life of the carpeting by about one-third to one-half. You can get very satisfactory pads made of felt, hair, a combination of hair and jute, or hair and jute mixed with foam. Rubber padding is available in either foam or sponge and should be about one-quarter inch thick.

Know the carpeting fibers

Law requires that carpeting be labeled to tell the fibers it contains as well as their percentages. When you buy rugs and carpeting cut from the rolls, the fiber content must be noted on your sales slip or invoice. Choose the fiber that suits your needs, because the fiber is an important part of your cost:

Wool is durable, soil-resistant, generally crushproof. Prices are medium to high. Better grades are mothproofed. But check this with the salesman.

Nylon is durable, resists crushing, spotting, abrasions, cleans easily. Generally rated the sturdiest of the man-made fabrics and priced about the same as wool.

Acrylic is a bit less durable than wool or nylon but costs less and is rated a good buy. It is often combined with other fibers. Better grades resemble wool.

Cotton and rayon, generally in low-priced carpets, rate poor to fair in durability and soil resistance. They might be the best buy for bedrooms and other low-traffic areas.

Save on stairway carpeting

Stair carpeting is nice to have but expensive, and it needs long-lasting quality. Try covering the stair treads with carpet samples in shades of a single color or in a variety of colors that complement one another. Samples are inexpensive. You can use a stencil to decorate the risers in one or more colors. If you do decide to carpet, order a bit more than you need so that you can tuck a section under, then shift the carpeting once it begins to show wear.

Where the values are

Many department stores run rug sales in August, January and February and you can expect savings of 25 percent or more. All year around most stores hold sales of roll ends, odd lots and mill closeouts; these are often the biggest bargains of them all.

Specialty rug houses outside the city limits sometimes take the lowest regular markups. But do comparative-shopping first.

Discount houses generally offer excellent values, though prices may not be any lower than those at department store sales, which may include the delivery and installation charges. At discount houses, ask if you have to pay extra.

You can sometimes get good carpeting buys at auctions or secondhand stores, but inspect them for damages. You'll have to pay for delivery, installation, probably for rug cleaning. Beware of:

1. A high markup on padding to compensate for the sale price of the carpet.

2. Advertisements that offer to carpet a room for a spectacularly low price—often a ploy to get the salesman into your home so he can talk you into high-cost carpeting.

3. Offers to install carpeting on a rental basis with no down payment, no financing charge, no cost for padding or installation and whatever rental you pay applied to any future purchase of either the original or the new carpet. The salesman will then show you how it would be cheaper to buy the carpeting than to rent it over any reasonable length of time. So you may as well shop around.

4. Salesmen who compute more yardage than you need.

5. Salesmen who insist that a carpet has special back-

ing and doesn't need separate padding. There is no such animal.

6. The substitution of a less expensive rug or carpet for the one you order and pay for. Make careful note of the specifications. Ask for a small swatch of the carpeting to compare with what is delivered.

Know the new smooth surface coverings

Vinyl and linoleum rolls come 6 feet wide and up to 100 feet long. They can be installed with a minimum of seams, but you'll probably need a professional to do the job. Tiles you can install yourself, saving labor costs. There's less waste than with sheet materials, and you can replace worn areas, tile by tile, without removing the entire floor.

Vinyl asbestos tile, widely used, is inexpensive and easy to install.

Vinyl sheet, a bit expensive, is durable, easy to care for.

Linoleum sheet costs less than vinyl but wears less well.

Cork tile is not recommended for heavy traffic areas— kitchens and foyers—although it is quiet and comfortable.

When you buy springs and mattresses

Many department stores sell mattresses under their own name. These cost far less than the national brands and they are identical. In fact, they are made by the national brand manufacturers for the store. Ask the salesman about them.

Medium-priced mattresses cost from $35 to $55, expensive ones from $90 to $110, and you find both innerspring and foam in all price ranges. An innerspring mattress is made of padding and insulating material on both sides of a coil unit. To last, it needs an adequate number of coils, properly tied, made of a good gauge of steel. The insulating materials are as important as the coils. In general, the more horsehair a mattress has, the better. Cheaper mattresses are usually filled with sisal pads and cotton felt.

Foam mattresses—either latex rubber or urethane—are moldproof, good for people who tend to have allergies; such mattresses do not have to be turned, as an innerspring does. Latex foam has better compression resistance and bounces back better than less expensive urethane foam. But urethane foam lasts well and will be a better buy for a bed in a playroom that is not used too often, or for a youth bed.

Mattresses come "firm," "super-firm" and "extra-firm." Test them by lying down on them, in the store, for several minutes; never mind how other shoppers stare. Sit on the edge too, to see if the mattress is as firm at the sides as in the center. Vertically stitched sides will help prevent sagging.

Buy the right bedsprings

Most stores offer mattresses together with box springs. Although you can buy the mattress alone, it may be the wrong economy. If your old box spring starts to sag, which it is bound to do eventually, your new mattress will sag, too.

Remember that foam mattresses come 4 to 6 inches shallower than innersprings. If you buy one you'll need an extra high box spring, to raise the bed to standard height.

You'll find three types of bedsprings at most stores: box springs, metal coil and flat.

Box springs are the most expensive but the most durable. Because the coils, upholstered with cotton felt or hair are covered with ticking, they do not collect dust and don't leave rust stains on the mattress or tear the mattress with protruding wire ends.

Metal coil springs cost less, but they need frequent cleaning, may rust and are apt to sag. They are not padded and usually not covered.

Flat springs don't cost much, but don't last long either. Sagging is the problem. You can extend the life of a flat spring by using an inexpensive plywood bedboard which is also good for the sleeper's back.

A good mattress and bedspring should last about ten years with proper care. Discount stores usually offer savings of 15 percent or more, but you may do much better at department store sales. No matter where you buy, be wary of:

1. "Lifetime guarantees."

2. Salesmen who push one item above all others and may get a bonus from the store or manufacturer for it.

3. Salesmen who try to switch you from the on-sale item to something else. At reliable stores, the on-sale items are your best value.

Learn about linens

Those fancy printed bed linens look glamorous in the magazines, but they end up being more expensive and more trouble than solids because you need to worry about fading and about harmonizing them with other colors at home. Also, you may find you prefer the more restful, less expensive and more versatile solids. The least expensive color is usually spanking clean white. Why pay more?

The fine weaves are expensive and don't wear as well as the better muslins. If you have young children, who are rough on sheets, use muslins. If you want a softer "feel," use percale for the pillows only.

To cut linen laundry bills, consider the permanent press linens. They're more expensive, but you soon start saving if you can put them through your own washing machine, then just smooth and fold them before putting them on your linen shelf.

You will launder more gently than the outside laundry does, so they will last longer. Always store the most recently laundered sheet or pillowcase on the bottom of the pile on your linen shelf, and take from the top when you change your bed linens. The rotation spreads the wear, helps linens last longer.

The luxury towels that look so pretty in ads are too expensive for your needs, especially with young children who are hard on towels. The discount houses offer attractive gay prints that will meet your requirements at better prices.

Learn furniture quality

When you buy furniture you buy a pig in a poke because the basic value of furniture lies under cover—*under* the finish or veneer of wood pieces, and *under* the fabrics of upholstered furniture. The least expensive item can become the most expensive in the long run if the veneer peels, the finish splits, if springs sag or doors warp. Buy the best you can afford, in the reliable stores, piece by piece. It's slow work, but you save money in the end.

Before buying wood furniture:

Check the finish. Inexpensive furniture that has been dipped, sprayed or coated in one process won't look new for very long. The finish on fine furniture may require as many as 25 steps, some of them done by hand. If the salesman can't tell you about this, ask to talk to the buyer.

Test chairs and tables for wobbly legs. If the salesman tells you it's the floor that is uneven, make him move the piece of furniture somewhere else.

See if doors and drawers open and close easily. Look for signs of warping. Don't let the salesman tell you that a stiff drawer or door will "ease up." It will probably get worse.

Check wood joinings. They should be firm. A well-made drawer has four dovetailed joints, preferably with small wooden blocks glued and screwed in each corner for reinforcement. The joinings that hold outer frames together should be glued, not nailed.

Hardwoods—walnut, teak, birch, mahogany, cherry, maple, oak—are what you can expect in fine-quality furniture. Softwoods—redwood, pine, cypress, cedar—cost less and are less durable, but don't pass them up for ready-to-finish or outdoor pieces.

"Solid wood" furniture is made of planks of wood ½ inch to 1¼ inch thick that are glued together. "Veneered" furniture means several layers of good-grade plywood laminated together, with a hardwood used for the outside. Most wood furniture on the market today is veneer plywood over a hardwood frame. The combination offers less warping, swelling and shrinking, plus greater strength and styling flexibility.

Before buying upholstered furniture, remember:

The frame. It must be strong enough to hold the spring construction, cushions and upholstery fabric firmly in place. Check that it is corner-blocked, glued, double-doweled, screwed for extra reinforcement and made of seasoned, kiln-dried wood.

The base. This should have strips of jute webbing woven across the bottom of the frame. Each strip should be fastened to the frame with closely spaced webbing nails or staples. Metal strips may be attached to the outside.

The springs. A chair needs at least 12 springs and a sofa needs 27 to prevent sagging. They should be securely hand-tied eight times—twice each from front to back, side to side, and diagonally both ways.

The insulating material. It goes over the springs and should be anchored well to the side rails, to add firmness and prevent the filling from slipping into the springs. Burlap, felted cotton, sisal or hair pads are commonly used.

The cushioning and filler. The better-quality materials include down, horsehair, rubber latex, polyurethane foam, fiberfill, kapok or a combination of any two. You won't get as much wear from moss, tow, sisal and excelsior. Test a cushion for pliability by squeezing it with your hand. If it doesn't bounce right back to its original shape, you can be sure it won't take much sitting, either.

POINTS TO REMEMBER

1. Use imagination and do-it-yourself techniques to "face-lift" secondhand furniture pieces.

2. Buy only what you need, but make it the best you can afford. Never buy without comparison-shopping first.

3. Learn to test good workmanship in the construction of furniture and in carpeting.

4. Hunt for opportunities offered by thrift shops, Salvation Army warehouses and auctions. Some discount houses offer big savings; so do clearance centers of large suburban stores.

Chapter Five

WHEN YOU BUY APPLIANCES

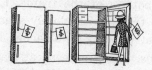

Appliances are expensive to start with, and every new one brings your electricity or gas bill up. Buy only what you absolutely need. Compare prices. Try to arrange demonstrations. Ask the salesman plenty of questions. Ask your friends who own the brand you plan to buy.

When you must buy, see if last year's model won't serve you just as well as this year's—it will probably cost less.

An appliance's design and styling generally have little to do with its serviceability. Why pay extra for a refrigerator with a pop-art painting on the door? It won't keep your food any fresher. A plain-looking electric broiler looks tinny next to one of the super-chrome models, but it will probably cook as efficiently and may be easier to clean.

The manufacturers usually offer their major appliances in three models—luxury, medium and low stripped-down versions. The stripped model can be a false economy if it cuts out important work-saving conveniences, since it is convenience that you buy in an appliance. A dryer, for example, may not be geared to handle the new materials you will put through it. A modern dryer should have cycles to dry the new no-press fabrics—or it wastes the money you will spend when you buy these.

The luxury machines often make you pay for more window dressing than you need. Usually the medium-priced models are the best buy in the long run.

The national-brand manufacturers often sell their appliances to chain stores, discount houses and department stores as private brands. The stores in turn sell the appliances under their own trade names—at savings to you. Salesmen will be happy to whisper that the washing machine or refrigerator was really made by so-and-so big company. It pays to ask.

You can get a secondhand appliance for as much as 50 percent off the original price. But insist on a guarantee of at least six months to a year.

Reconditioned appliances tend to cost more than secondhand ones. Reconditioning can mean anything from a complete overhaul to a new motor or just an outside paint job. Find out exactly what was done. Get an ironclad guarantee.

Wherever you buy an electrical appliance, it should carry an Underwriters' Laboratory Seal. A gas appliance should bear the seal of the American Gas Association. Study the terms of the guarantee or warranty carefully. Sign and send back the warranty card to the manufacturer, if you are asked to do so, in order to make the guarantee valid. Always keep the sales slip, which should be clearly dated.

Before you use the machine, take the time to read the instruction booklet carefully, in order to use it properly. Keep the instructions handy, close to the appliance, so that you can refer back to them conveniently whenever you have a question. This habit can save you the cost of many service calls.

Should you change fuel?

Whenever you buy a new major utility appliance, you will wonder whether to change fuel. Check the costs for gas and electricity in your area, and also how much you use of each kind throughout the house. Unit costs for fuel go down as you use more. It could cost you less to use all one type of fuel rather than divide your use among gas, oil and electricity.

But also check the cost of bringing in new fuel lines.

A woman may hanker for an electric oven, for example, but it can be expensive to bring in the proper voltage and wiring. Will the fuel lines add hundreds of dollars to the price of the appliance? The least expensive appliance change usually means buying one that uses the same fuel as the old one, and placing it in the same position.

Choosing a range

Since a housewife spends a large part of her day over a hot stove, she ought to have one she really likes.

Before deciding between a gas or electric range, check the utility rates in your area. If there is a significant difference and if you have no deep personal prejudice, choose the type that will be cheapest to operate. Gas and electricity cook with equal speed and efficiency—once you get used to the oven, and assuming it is in good working order. Here are the types offered now:

Built-in ranges, designed with the rest of the kitchen according to a master plan, are generally attractive but expensive to install. Replacement is costly because of carpenter work involved. They usually can't be taken along, should you move.

Stack-ons sit on top of a counter or storage cabinet and can be designed to look built-in. Installation is less costly, too.

Drop-in ranges, know also as set-ins, consist of a cooking top and under-counter oven and fit between two counters. They are attractive and less expensive to install than the conventional built-ins.

Double-deckers are designed to save space. One oven is stacked on top of another, with the burners in between. They are expensive, need installation and often do not allow good working space over the burners.

Freestanding ranges can have all the automatic conveniences of the new built-ins, without the high carpenter bills for installation. They are well enough insulated so that you can place cabinets against them for a built-in look.

You can get ranges with two separate ovens and six surface burners rather than the conventional four. A large family or a love of cooking might justify the additional expense. Otherwise don't get carried away by the vision of gracious living. You won't change your living patterns for the sake of the oven.

Some medium-to-upper-priced electric and gas ranges come with a thermostatically controlled burner; when the food has reached the desired temperature, the flame or electricity is automatically reduced. It is a luxury item you won't often use. Why pay for it, unless you have a specific need for it?

In many ranges an automatic timer can be set to turn the oven on, cook the food for a preset time and turn the oven off when it is done. This is helpful when a wife works.

In recent years several manufacturers have come out with ovens that clean themselves. You set a control and exceptionally high oven heat does the rest. It is a great worksaver, but expensive. Many new chemical oven cleaners are making it easier to clean ovens manually.

How fancy a dishwasher?

It will cost you about six cents for electricity per cycle to run a dishwasher. You can get an economy washer with three cycles—for rinsing, washing and drying. Or, as the prices go up, with several rinse, wash-and-dry cycles, plus special cycles for pots, fine china, stemware, plate-warming as well as rinse-and-hold (if you don't want to wash right away). A machine in the middle range is your best buy, will offer useful conveniences but not luxury frills you will rarely need.

The nearer a dishwasher is placed to the sink, the less expensive the installation, because of plumbing requirements; also, the more convenient to use. Portable models are wheeled to the sink at washing time and connected to the faucet with a hose. They can save you the cost of extensive remodeling in order to make space for a built-in beside the sink. If you remodel later, or move, most portables can also be installed in a permanent position beside the sink.

That new refrigerator

Refrigerator prices range from about $160 to over $600. Your best buy is probably somewhere in between. The type of refrigerator you need depends on the size of your family, whether you store more fresh food or frozen, and whether you already have, or expect to buy, a separate freezer.

The lowest-priced full-sized models have one outside door with the freezer at the top of the unit but relatively small. This is not recommended for long-term freezing.

Combination refrigerator-freezers are becoming more popular. Prices range from moderate to high. Most of these have two outside doors and the freezer compartment may be above, below or to the side. It has its own temperature control and will hold food for up to one year.

The price you pay also depends on how much work you want to save and how many gadgets you have to have.

Lower-priced refrigerators must be defrosted manually. You turn the dial to defrost, and empty the pan when it fills with water.

Refrigerators that defrost automatically cost more. Periodic thawing keeps the frost from accumulating; the water runs into a pan which does not have to be emptied but must be cleaned fairly often.

Frost-free refrigerators are the most work-saving and the most expensive. They produce air currents that prevent ice from forming on the coils or on food in the freezer compartment. If a wife works outside the home, it may be an economy to free her from this regular heavy chore, as well as from other big home chores that would make her outside employment impossible.

The door shelves in refrigerators are handy for small jars and give you lots more usable space. But if you like gadgets you can pay for more than you need. The price goes up with the extras, so judge them carefully.

Covered vegetable crispers, for example, keep your produce fresher. An automatic ice-cube maker is very practical if you entertain a great deal, but it's not that much more trouble to empty and refill ice trays yourself. A special high-temperature compartment will keep your butter more spreadable; you can also remember to take the spread out of the refrigerator before you make the toast. You can pay for swing-out shelves in the refrigerator and pullout baskets in the freezer. Or you can stick your hand in for a minute and save a little money.

Do you need a freezer?

If your family is small, and if you have a good-sized refrigerator-freezer combination, you may not need a separate freezer. With a large family, or if you shop infrequently, or if a wife works or likes to cook several meals at one time, the freezer can be a good investment—especially if you want to stock up on meat and frozen foods when you find good buys.

Upright freezers are more convenient to use and usually cost more than the chest type. If you hunt carefully, though, you can find an upright at a good price. Also, an upright may be frost-free while all chest types must be defrosted manually, a time-consuming and messy job.

All manufacturers offer a guarantee against spoiled food for 48 hours after a power cutoff due to mechanical or structural failure, but read the conditions on the guarantee. Usually the door must be unopened and the maker notified within 24 hours. Freezers come with a variety of extras: a signal that warns you if the electricity goes off; built-in defrost drains; interior lights; adjustable shelves; automatic door locks and quick-freeze shelves. Buy only the features that are important to you.

Choose the right washing machine

You can buy a good medium-priced washer for between $210 and $260. A single-speed machine will cost you less, but it won't be nearly as satisfactory for today's synthetics, the wash-and-wear, durable press and other modern fabrics. At the other extreme, a luxury model costing about $400 may offer only a more complicated system of controls. Don't buy the fancy twists you don't really need and which only mean more controls that may break down. Look for the following features:

1. At least two agitation speeds—normal and slow.

2. Flexibility in wash-and-rinse water temperature.

3. More than one fill level, to save water when you wash small loads.

4. A soak or prewash cycle.

5. Either a fabric-softener dispenser or a bleach dispenser.

6. A lint filter that is easily accessible to you for cleaning.

The less supervision a washer needs, the more it will free the user for other jobs. Here are the four general types now offered:

The fully automatic washer fills itself with water, washes, rinses, extracts water and stops—with one turn of a control. Front-loading automatics need less water than most of the new top-loaders, but they cannot handle as large a load of wash.

The semiautomatic washer looks like an automatic, but you have to reset the controls for each phase of the wash-rinse-spin cycles. It costs less than an automatic but needs more attention.

Wringer and spinner washers use less water than the other types and are less expensive. They need separate tubs for washing and rinsing and must be filled manually, using a hose connected to the faucets of a sink.

Washer-dryer combinations save space. But the housewife can't wash while drying, or dry while washing, so laundering takes longer. When the washer must be replaced you are forced to get a new dryer, too. Separate machines may be more economical in the long run.

Buy a dryer for new fabrics

You've probably invested in clothing that is wash-and-wear or durable press. It pays to buy a dryer designed to cope with them. Time-and-temperature controlled dryers, either gas or electric, allow you to choose the drying time that is best for the type of fabric and size of the load. Some models have a cool-off drying cycle, and a cycle with *no* heat, for certain synthetics.

Gas dryers are more expensive than electric ones but, because of lower utility rates in most areas, they are less expensive to operate.

Be sure the machine has an easy-to-get-at lint filter, and clean this often, to avoid service calls. Also look for a safety device that automatically stops the action when the door is opened.

You don't necessarily need a dryer with a foot pedal for opening the door when your hands are full, one with an air-freshener device built in, or with a light in the drum to help you find small items that get flattened against the inside. These are extras. Can you work around them? For example, you don't need a light to find small things if you dry them in a mesh bag.

How about last year's air conditioner?

The cooling capacity of an air conditioner used to be measured in tonnage. Now home models are in British Thermal Units (BTUs). The number of BTUs determines how much heat a unit can remove from a room in one hour. To figure the BTUs you need to:

1. Measure the room to be cooled by height, width, length.

2. Figure out for how many hours direct sunlight enters the room, and from which direction.

3. Note whether the room is directly under the roof or not.

4. Estimate the number of people generally using the room.

5. Take the information to the dealer who will compute the BTUs.

Before you invest in a machine, what are your voltage requirements? Models using 75 amperes or less can be plugged directly into household outlets that operate on 115 volts. If the unit uses more than 75 amperes, you will need to put in a separate voltage circuit—an expensive operation.

Buy your air conditioner out of season to get a better price. Last year's model may be just as good as this year's, and much cheaper. Hunt for a dealer who has some left over.

Make certain the unit has an easily removable filter, and plan to wash or vacuum it after every 100 hours or so.

If you find a big price difference among air conditioners with the same BTU capacity, it means you are paying for extra features. Ask what they are. Some are worth it, some not.

Quietness, especially in bedrooms, is worth every extra cent.

A unit that is adaptable to through-the-wall installation, in case you don't want to obstruct your window view, may not be necessary. Models are made today to fit just about every type of window, so don't let yourself be talked into something "special" that is more expensive. You can probably find a regular model designed for your needs.

Some air conditioners come with front wood panels to blend with your decor, or with fancy cabinet doors to cover everything. Some homeowners like the disguise; others prefer the honest functional look. In any event, the disguise raises the price and doesn't give you any better cooling. Why pay for it?

How fancy TV?

The more parts any appliance has, the more likely it is to need repairs. A television set has about 20 tubes, 1,000 components and 2,000 or 3,000 connections. Obviously, you'll have to figure on paying for a few repairs during the life of your TV set. Hunt carefully and ask friends for recommendations when you use a TV repairman. Don't let young children play with the controls.

Color sets break down more easily and cost more to repair than black and white models, in addition to being more expensive to begin with. Do you have to have color?

The more elaborate the cabinet, the higher the price, but the show is the same. You can save money and get an attractive effect by fitting a lower-priced portable TV set into a bookshelf or into an inexpensive cabinet you own. The portables are handsome; in fact they are usually better-looking than the manufacturer's cabinets just because they are simple and functional. Put a portable on an inexpensive low table you can paint yourself, and enjoy its simple good looks out in the open.

New kinds of vacuum cleaners

Upright vacuums generally do the best cleaning job on carpeting and rugs. Canister-tank type models are usually better for above-the-floor cleaning—for furniture, venetian blinds, etc. However, you don't need both kinds. In recent years, manufacturers of uprights have improved the above-the-floor efficiency of their equipment. Canister-makers have also made progress on their rug-cleaning functions. It could boil down to which type of vacuum feels more comfortable to push and pull around.

Lightweight vacuums, known also as electric brooms, are no substitute for full-sized models but are effective for floor and rug touch-ups. Weighing as little as seven or eight pounds, they are easier to bring out of a closet than the big models, and far more efficient than a carpet sweeper. They are more expensive than sweepers, however. Consider carefully whether you need one if you don't have carpeting in heavily used areas.

Before buying any vacuum cleaner, make sure that:

1. The dust bag empties easily.
2. The suction is adequate for your type of rug.
3. The cord is long enough for maneuvering.

4. The machine doesn't tip over at a slight tug.

5. The floor attachment is properly shaped to fit under furniture.

When you buy small appliances

Toasters. Many manufacturers have been working on eye appeal, but you pay a higher price for their "art." More important than appearance is capacity. A six-slice toaster may save precious time if you're feeding a large family a quick breakfast. Get one with a crumb tray that can be easily removed for cleaning. Some toasters have wider wells for muffins and rolls, which means no more having to dig them out. Most come with a wide range of dark-to-light settings. Pay only for function.

Irons. Modern irons have non-stick sole plates, but they need care to avoid scratched surfaces from buttons and zippers. Many models now have heat settings for synthetics and wash-and-wear.

If you buy a steam or steam-spray iron, get one that uses plain water from the tap. The irons that need distilled water are inconvenient and buying distilled water or a filter means added expense that continues for the life of the iron.

Electric frypans. Besides frying, those with well-controlled thermostats also simmer and roast, if the meat is first seared.

Many electric fryers now come with non-stick surfaces and with high dome covers to take roasts. A square pan gives more cooking area than a round one of the same width. Get one with a removable plug and control, so that the pan itself can be immersed in water for cleaning.

An electric frypan can serve as an extra burner, but to make it worth the cost you should have good counter space in order to use it often.

Electric coffee makers. Some of the low-priced models do not indicate the fill level for water. You will have to measure out the water with a cup. All coffeepots should be fully immersable; a poorly cleaned pot makes poor-tasting coffee.

Before you buy: do you really require an electric model? Large-capacity electric urns are a convenience for entertaining a huge party, but a warming tray can keep your regular pot at the right serving temperature—for family use and for small gatherings.

Electric mixers. Look for a mixer that has a good blade and a wide range of speeds. Some have attachments for grinding meat, juicing, etc. Think about how often you are likely to use these. Chances are that the attachments will just take up shelf space. Why pay extra for them?

Blenders. The higher-priced models offer numerous speeds and an automatic timer that turns the blender on and off. Some now have new low speeds that permit cream whipping or beating egg white. You can get one that even heats food, but again, don't buy what you don't need. A blender should have: a large enough container, stainless steel blades, parts that are easily removable for cleaning, a pouring spout and a two-part cover that can be used as a measuring cup.

POINTS TO REMEMBER

1. Disregard fancy design and styling in any appliance, from refrigerator to toaster: they merely increase price, but not serviceability, sometimes not even the item's appearance.

2. It might pay to shop around for secondhand and reconditioned appliances; some cost only 50 percent of the original price. But try to get a good guarantee—at least six months to a year.

3. Check fuel supply needs (gas and/or electricity) before you change over from the one to the other: unit costs for fuel go *down* as you use *more*.

4. Find out—*before* you buy—if you really need that multi-gadget refrigerator, food freezer, brand-new air conditioner (when last year's model, cheaper, will do) or overornate color TV set-cum-cabinet.

5. Don't go overboard on eye appeal of small appliances such as electric irons, frypans, coffee makers, mixers and blenders. Simple, functional style often looks better, works just as well.

Chapter Six

YOUR
CAR
DOLLAR

After your home and the children's education, your car is probably the biggest single family expenditure you are likely to make. The minute you drive a car from the dealer's garage toward your own, it starts losing its value—35 percent the first year, 20 percent the second and 15 percent the third—and you can't do anything about that loss. It makes dollar sense to keep a car in the best possible condition and also to keep a tight rein on the cost of maintaining and operating it.

The big car users who run fleets of taxis and rental cars have a very simple motto: NEVER NEGLECT A SMALL REPAIR. Here is why:

A five-dollar wheel alignment can save a $50 pair of tires; a one-dollar carburetor adjustment can save that much in gas every time you fill your tank (and you know how many times you do that!).

The most obvious upkeeping is washing and waxing. It may sound strange, but a clean car is usually a safe car. In the racing world the highest praise a car can receive is to be called "sanitary." Keeping it clean helps prevent body rusting and keeps down wear and tear on interior rugs and upholstery, which boost a car's resale value.

If you learn to tackle these small repairs yourself you don't have to pay big money to servicemen. First, arm yourself with the proper tools. A pair of pliers, two screwdrivers (one straight and one Phillips) and an adjustable wrench are all you really need. You're not going to take the car apart and put it together again, only tighten up those loose screws and bolts, tuck in that piece of carpet and screw it down or replace a burned-out headlight.

If you are handy with tools and want to do more, there are several good repair manuals on the market which, coupled with a good set of wrenches and sockets, will give you step-by-step repair instructions for almost any job that doesn't call for an automotive engineering degree.

When you're on your own, stop reading those ads offering lifetime spark plugs, pills to boost your gas mileage,"flow-through" muffler systems and the myriad of products claiming they will make your car run and sound better. The only thing they do is separate you from your hard-earned cash, and if you're not on your toes, they will do a splendid job of that.

Save on gas, oil, antifreeze

Saving money on the operation of your car is unglamorous and unexciting: pulling away from a stoplight smoothly and evenly, cruising down a highway at a steady speed, often below the posted speed limit. But remember, your gas tank is where the big saving is. If you drive 12,000 miles a year and get an extra three miles per gallon of gas, which is easy, you save $360. That's not some accountant's $360. It's money that never left your pocket!

If you're going to put one of those humorous plaques on your dashboard, it should read: NEVER DO ANYTHING SUDDENLY. Every time you jam on your brakes, a cash register rings somewhere. Every time you floor the accelerator, some gas station owner smiles. Every time you turn a corner with your tires squealing, a salesman starts counting his commission. The list can go on indefinitely. It's a very expensive list—and that's *your money*.

Unless your car requires it, never use premium gas. Contrary to the old wives' tale, you get no added gas mileage. Use of premium, in fact, could lead to premature burning of the engine's exhaust valves. On the basis of 12,000 miles a year, the use of premium could cost you an extra $350.

Never let the gas level go below one quarter full. All gases, including the extra filtered kind, contain impurities. These, coupled with water condensation in your gas tank, if drawn through could damage the fuel pump or dirty the carburetor. The fuel pump would have to be repaired, and the dirty carburetor would cut heavily into your gas mileage. It helps if you use some of the so-called dry gas additive at least twice a year, and you should definitely use it just before the winter season.

Don't bother using the expensive multi-grade oils. Oils come in various "weights," but all you need is a small "weight" type. A detergent 20-weight oil (price—⅓ less than the multi-grades) is perfect for most of the year, 30-weight for very hot climates and 10-weight should do well for cold winter areas.

Even the newest cars, with their long periods between oil changes, need an oil change at least four times a year. Make sure the filter is replaced regularly. It's your first line of defense against a dirty engine.

Don't throw out your antifreeze when winter is over. If you have storage space and a can, save it for the next winter. If not, just leave it in the car all year round. As winter comes on, ask the gas station attendant to check the protection level and top up your radiator with new antifreeze.

Save tires

Rotate your tires. Front tires wear much faster than the rears. The spare will never wear, unless you get it on the road. Rotating your tires is one job you can do yourself without too much trouble.

Use this system: put one of the front tires in the trunk for the spare. Bring the rears diagonally to the front (right rear to left front, left rear to right front). Put the old spare and the other front on the rear, and you're set.

Never let your tires get underinflated. If anything, the tires should be inflated a pound or so above the manufacturer's recommendation. If the maker gives a range, inflate your tires to the upper end of the range.

Every time you get a chance, check your tires. Get small stones and pieces of road debris out of the tread, and make sure there are no cuts or bubbles in the tire wall. If you remove the stones from the tread before they have a chance to get imbedded, you may save a tire replacement.

After about 20,000 miles, when the time comes to replace your regular tires, if the budget can stand it and you plan to keep your car for another two years, consider the new belted tread tires. They are more expensive (almost double in some cases) but more than worth it, since they last more than twice as long, are safer and allow the driver greater control. They have drawbacks: they're slightly noisier and give a harder ride, but the average driver won't notice either after the first 100 miles.

When the serviceman comes to you with some part in his hand and says, "You need a new grammis, and it'll cost you all you've got," ask him about a rebuilt part. These are as good as new, since in most cases factory parts are used in the rebuilding. The generator or fuel pump or carburetor, or whatever, is taken apart and cleaned. All worn parts are replaced with new ones and put together again. Only the frame, cover and metal parts are reused, since they are almost never damaged. The price is often half of what a new part would cost.

Save on car insurance

Your biggest single maintenance outlay is the cost of insuring your car. Here, too, there are ways of saving big money.

There are five key kinds of auto insurance: liability, medical, collision, comprehensive and uninsured motorist coverage.

1. *Liability* insurance protects you against any body in-

jury and property damage judgments for which you may become liable.

2. *Medical* plans pay for hospital and doctor bills for you and your passengers in any accident.

3. *Collision* insurance pays for repairing your car after a collision or vandalism.

4. *Comprehensive* coverage insures you against loss of the car from fire, theft and many forms of natural occurrences.

5. *Uninsured motorist* plans cover you against some costs in which an uninsured or hit-and-run driver may be liable for damages.

There are two different kinds of insurance companies—stock and mutual.

A stock company is owned by a group of stockholders and sells its insurance through independent brokers. These brokers sell many different "brands" of insurance. They will shop around to find the best plan for you and serve as your agent.

Mutual companies are owned by their customers. Profits are distributed among the "owners" in the form of lower rates. The drawback is that you buy your insurance from an employee of the insurance company and *you* have to do the shopping around.

But buying from a mutual company will pay: mutual insurance is often as much as 20 percent cheaper than stock insurance.

All insurance costs are based on percentage of risk, and auto insurance is no exception. The underwriters estimate in advance what their costs may be for settlements, etc., and set their rates high enough to pay for them. To figure their risk, they develop three "profiles"—one of the driver, the second of the location where the driving will be done, and the third involving the kind of driving that will be done.

You cannot change your location and kind of driving, but you can do a lot about the driver.

For example: most insurance companies have a rating

system for drivers. You get a number of points for each chargeable accident, moving violation or claim you make or have made on you. They add this on top of a base rate. For one point—a reportable accident with damages, or a claim over $100, or a speeding ticket—you pay the base rate plus a 5 percent surcharge. For two points you pay the base rate plus a 50 percent surcharge. For three points the surcharge goes up to 100 percent and for four or more it's a staggering 150 percent.

By that time you may find it difficult to become insured. In states that have compulsory insurance laws it means you are either a pedestrian or a passenger.

When a teen-age driver uses your car, expect the rate to go up steeply. If you have an under-25-year-old male driver in the house you'll be paying a base rate three times higher, for instance. But if he takes a driver education course in school, you can cut this surcharge in half. That can be a savings of $100 in high-rate areas.

If you drive more than ten miles a day, to and from work, try to take public transportation or get into a car pool—with someone else's car. Your surcharge is 40 to 50 percent. When you can eliminate it, that's another $100 saved—and you've stretched your car dollar further.

Renting isn't cheaper

There is a new fad—car renting. Some may tell you it's cheaper. Some ads about it sound great: pay a flat sum each month, like auto payments, and forget the rest. No insurance, no repairs, and if the car breaks down, we lend you one while we fix it.

But unless you drive great distances each year—20,000 miles or more—or use a car for business, you will find it hard to put your finger on any money saved. Take a close, long look at these plans. You *may* be able to save on one of them, but the odds are not in your favor.

Like insurance, rental charges are based on percentage of risk. You may be a careful, safe driver who takes care of his car, but you may end up paying for the repairs of someone who isn't. Some plans let you pay for insurance or repairs, and are lower-priced. What you are doing, in effect, is buying the car without getting it. When you finish paying for a car you buy, you have at least—for better or worse—a car of your own.

Businessmen and salesmen find that renting cars is a good way to keep track of their expenses for tax purposes. The average driver doesn't need to pay for that privilege.

Save when you buy a new car

If you're going out to buy a new car, remember that the road is full of pitfalls. Four overall rules are:

1. Never buy more car than you need (this can save you an extra $1,000 by the time you're finished).

2. Watch out how you finance the car (more on this later).

3. Don't try to keep up with the Joneses (you can't because they just got a bequest, which they blew on the car but didn't tell you about).

4. Most important, buy only those EXTRA COST options which you feel you absolutely can't get along without.

Manufacturers list prices don't mean much any more. They serve as a starting point for the bargaining. Discounts of 10 percent are not uncommon. Every so often a salesman will offer more than that to get one particular car off the floor. Some people get an extra $100 or so chopped off the price just to take a car painted an odd color.

An automobile is only a tool to carry you from where you are to where you must go, comfortably, at the lowest cost. Everything else is extraneous. Don't pay for it.

Before you go out to buy, you should ask yourself two questions:

What will you be carrying in the car? What kind of driving do you do? The answer to the first dictates the shape of the car you need. The answer to the second tells what else goes into the car.

The car shape that fits most needs is the standard two- or four-door sedan. For easy entry, accessibility, general all-around looks and price this style is unbeatable. All the full-sized sedans (the compacts, too, since there's little real difference in size anymore) have as much inside car space as anyone will need. Except for when a family travels with a week's luggage, it's highly doubtful that the trunk will ever be filled.

The two- or four-door sedan is also the least expensive and nowadays is as stylish as most of the hardtops that are on the market.

If you have a large family of more than three children, or carry bulky boxes often, the station wagon should be your choice. There are models for all pocketbooks, ranging from small (about $2400) to the big boys (around $4000).

A three-seat wagon will cost an extra $110, but if your cargo is people, it is worth it. If you tow a boat or trailer, make sure you get the towing suspension option, which is also available on sedans. It will save lots of tire and suspension wear, and it's safer too. Even if you don't tow, it pays to buy the option because it cuts down on the wallowing some wagons develop when traveling at high speed while empty. It costs only $15 to $20.

If you don't mind a car that looks like a truck, consider Ford, Chevy or Dodge. They offer van-type wagons, the shape made famous by VW's Micro-Bus, but with U.S. power. They run between $2300 and $2600, depending on the model that you select.

America's best-selling styles are the hardtops and "personal" cars. These look more attractive, but for that extra beauty—and there isn't that much extra anymore—you pay two prices. First, the car costs more—from $20 to more than $200 over the basic price. Luxury interiors and bigger engines are also standard, boosting the price even more. If you want a car without the extra doodads you have to put in a special order and wait several months.

Secondly, with all the power assists and bigger engines

these cars cost more to run. Furthermore, interior and trunk space are often sacrificed in the interests of style.

Buy the right engine

Don't buy more engine power than you need. Here's a good rule of thumb: for low speed, stop-and-go driving, as in the city or the suburbs, you need a small engine for economy. It should run at fairly high revolutions, for power, so that you always have "zoom" for emergencies. For high-speed turnpike driving, you need a powerful, fairly slow-turning engine that will have a long life.

With cars now weighing from 3500 to 5000 pounds, any engine that doesn't deliver at least 120 hp is underpowered. If you plan to get any power options, you have to step up a bit. But remember, don't overbuy. The bigger the engine, the bigger the fuel and maintenance bills.

Save on the transmission

There are five varieties of transmission: 3-speed standard, 3-speed with overdrive, 4-speed manual, 2-speed automatic and 3-speed automatic.

The 3-speed standard is the most economical to buy and operate. When you add overdrive you boost the price often as much as an automatic would cost. Unless you plan on doing more than 30,000 miles of high-speed driving, you'll never make up in gas saving what you paid for the overdrive. Your main saving is still in your gas tank.

The 4-speed option is a waste. It was designed for racing or sports-type cars which have small engines with a narrow power range. Since American cars have a broad power range, to order this is pure show.

If you do a lot of city driving, it may be convenient to specify one of the two-speed automatics. But you'll have to pay from $150 to $185 for it, and you'll lose as much as 5 miles per gallon of gas. That's a stiff price for this kind of convenience.

The 3-speed automatics give better acceleration, smoother shifting, higher cruising speeds and slightly better mileage. But they cost more—$225 and up. They aren't available, in most cases, on lower-price car models.

Power steering, in these days of heavier cars and wider tires, is becoming more of a necessity and less of a luxury. It adds about $100 to the cost of the car. Don't let the salesman talk you up to a bigger motor for it. Unless you live in the mountains, where a V-8 is necessary, the bigger 6-cylinder engines are powerful enough.

Be wary of used cars

If you're going out into the used-car jungle, beware. Be forearmed. Have a mechanic you trust check out any car you choose. Any reputable dealer will allow this, and if he doesn't, walk out.

In general, it's best to buy a Ford from a dealer who sells new Fords, a Chevy from a new Chevy dealer, etc. Such a car is more likely to be in top condition since the original owner was happy enough with it to buy another. The dealer thinks twice of his reputation before he'll put a "dog" on his lot. He will wholesale these off to other used-car dealers.

When you're looking at used cars, we suggest you use this checklist:

1. Examine the driver's seat. Is it badly worn? A worn driver's seat means high mileage.

2. Is tire wear even all around? If it is, the owner rotated his tires, a tipoff that the car received good care. Also, check the condition of the tires against the odometer. A good set of tires should last about 20,000 miles.

3. Look for rust. A good spot to check is the underside of the doors. Press hard on the bottom of the door. If there is any give, it means rust is starting to work on the inside of the door.

4. Open the trunk. Is it clean? Is there any rust? Was the inside of the trunk recently painted? Are there any weld marks? The latter two are signs of repair of body damage — beware. Are all the tools there, in their proper places?

5. Look closely underneath the car. If there are any oil leaks, forget the car, no matter what you are told.

6. If the car passes all the above tests, drive it around. Pick a rough street, to listen for rattles. Drive it up a hill or two to see if the engine pulls smoothly. Drive through a water puddle, then stop the car and check the track. Do the rear tires follow the fronts? If not, the car has been in a bad accident and the frame is bent. Don't buy.

7. After the car is thoroughly warmed up, check the exhaust. Is it heavy? Forget the car. It could mean expensive motor repairs. Check the temperature gauge. Is the level too high? The radiator has blockages and may have to be taken out and cleaned. And check again underneath for oil leaks.

8. Jam on the brakes once or twice. Does the car swerve to one side? Does the car stop easily, without judder (shaking *and* noise) and without a squeal?

9. Now, if the price seems right, call in your mechanic to *really* go over the car.

If your car budget is limited, don't rule out the foreign car. VW, Renault, Datsun and Sunbeam all put out excellent small family cars, under or close to the $2,000 level. Inside space may be limited, but they cost little to operate, and you can get major parts for them in the U.S. Besides the above, Opels are sold through Buick dealers. You can buy English Fords from Ford here.

Shop for financing

If you want to save big money, shop around for financing as much as you do for your car. Plan to pay off the loan as quickly as you can. The difference in interest charges alone between a 24-month and a 36-month loan is substantial. On a $2,000 loan at 6 percent advertised interest, for example, the difference in charges for the extra year is $180.

As a rule, dealer-offered finance plans are the most expensive. Plans offered by thrift institutions are cheaper, but even here some are better than others. In one city, for instance, one bank offers auto loans at $1 per $100 loan per year less than the others. On a $2,000 loan for three years, that's $60 in your pocket. In some states you can get loans on your savings account at a drastically reduced rate, sometimes as low as $2 per year per $100 of the loan.

POINTS TO REMEMBER

1. Never buy more car than you need, in terms of engine power, transmission, optional accessories. Watch your financing charges. Also consider some foreign makes (VW, Renault, etc.) that may be better suited to your budget.

2. Don't neglect small repairs. Learn to make minor repairs yourself by studying repair manuals and acquiring a good tool kit.

3. Save on gas and oil by smooth driving, even cruising. Your biggest savings are in your gas tank. You don't really need expensive multi-grade oils.

4. Rotate your tires because front tires wear much faster than rear ones. Never let them get underinflated. The new belted tread tires are twice as expensive but last more than twice as long.

5. One of your biggest outlays is for insurance. Shop around. Mutual insurance company policies are often 20 percent cheaper than stock company insurance.

Chapter Seven

YOUR
HOUSING
DOLLAR

Housing may represent your family's biggest expenditure. With judicious planning it can also become your best investment, but we will go into its investment value later. Here we will talk mainly about ways to stretch your dollar in running a home—whether it is your own house or a rental.

The time to start stretching your dollar in the operation of a home comes when you choose it. Once you find a community where you want to settle, study it over a period of time. Find out the going market prices for houses or apartments, and also whether prices change at different seasons. Plan to buy or rent when demand is lowest.

Know what you are spending

To stretch your dollar, choose a house that will be right for your pocketbook and inexpensive to run. If a house interests you, look into all the factors involved in the upkeep.

A checklist will help you to keep tabs on the cost of maintaining and refurbishing the home according to your budget and your needs. Ask the real estate broker who shows it, and the current owner, to give you a breakdown of the annual costs for taxes, heating, water, gardening, painting and so on.

Understanding taxes

If taxes in an area you like are high, find out why. Perhaps you are paying for land with high value because it's near water, or the community has a topnotch school system or fast transportation or other valuable community services. Such homes usually have a higher selling price. They may be worth the cost factor, but think it through.

If dollar-stretching must be your paramount consideration in housing, you might have to forgo the good schools or transportation or recreation facilities. Some services might not be necessities to your family. You will save in your purchase price and perhaps in taxes, but remember that when you come to sell, your house will not command as high a price as a comparable house in areas with more services.

Older communities generally have lower taxes because so many essential services have already been built and paid for. New communities have many advantages, but they do also have to tax in order to buy the basic services you want.

If you own property you can deduct real estate taxes, as well as mortgage interest, from your earned income, and this can give you a big income tax savings every year. A veteran can lower his real estate taxes on homes that are under a qualifying market value in certain states. Find out from your local tax collector what this means to you.

Negotiate the price coolly

How firm is a seller's asking price? The only way you can find out is by offering much less and then negotiating up, step-by-step, until you and the seller reach a meeting point.

Some people have gotten very good buys by offering an "outrageously" low price, especially when the house has been on the market for a long time or the previous owners have had to move quickly. The real estate broker can often indicate how much below the asking price your first offer should be.

Living with a mortgage

When you take out a mortgage you are buying the use of money, and like anything else, money costs money. You save dollars in total cost when you put down as much cash on a house as you can, when you incur as small a mortgage as you can, and when you pay it back as quickly as you can. Remember that interest is a function not only of the amount you borrow and of the rate of interest, but also of *time*.

If you can get the previous owner's mortgage transferred to you, you will find it a good buy if he bought it in a period when interest rates were lower. However, such a transfer is usually not possible. More typically, you have to secure your mortgage from a savings and loan association, commercial bank or mortgage banker.

Savings and loan associations, first established in 1831, are required by law to invest a great proportion of their funds in mortgage loans. They finance more houses than any other kind of lending institution, because they specialize in single-family homes. Several types of mortgage arrangements are available. Find out for which you qualify and which fits in best with your overall financial situation.

Because a home is a major family investment, it is a good idea to take out mortgage insurance so that if the wage earner dies, the property is transferred, free and clear, to the widow or other beneficiary. Many savings and loan associations offer mortgage life insurance plans that have low premiums as they qualify under group policy rates.

Insurance companies issue individual policies to homeowners for this purpose. Also, for a small added charge, a husband can protect himself against the risk of being unable to meet the house payments should his wife die, and he must hire a housekeeper or nurse for young children.

Save when you build

Before buying property on which to build, know what the neighborhood offers. Investigate schools, police and fire protection, and arrangements for garbage and sewage disposal. These services will affect your taxes. They should be available and should be good, too, when taxes are high. Look into the availability of churches, shops, doctors, hospitals and recreational facilities. Before you buy, ask a loan officer at a savings and loan association, or other lenders, about the land

MORGAGES

Here are the principal plans offered today:

Conventional loan. You probably will be required to pay ten or more percent of the appraised value or selling price of the house as a down payment. The more you pay down, the lower your total dollar cost for the mortgage loan.

FHA-insured mortgage. Your loan is insured by the Federal Housing Administration, which allows the lender to give you a higher percentage of the appraised value of the house than granted without the insurance feature.

Veterans Administration guaranteed mortgage (GI Loan). The Veterans Administration guarantees the lender a percentage of your loan. If you are a veteran, you may be entitled to a mortgage without making any down payment. The Veterans Administration will appraise the house for you, and in the event you wish to prepay your loan you do not have to pay any penalty. That can mean a savings of from 1 to 3 percent.

On all three types of loans you pay a fixed monthly amount during the term of the mortgage and, from it, the interest and amortization (loan repayment) are taken. Your interest is computed each month on the unpaid balance of the loan. Most of your payment goes for the interest at first. As your equity increases, the amount required for interest goes down and the sum for amortization goes up.

In addition to interest and amortization, the bills for taxes and insurance may be budgeted monthly and paid to the lender. If so, he pays these obligations as they become due.

Package mortgage. This mortgage includes payments for home appliances such as a dishwasher, dryer, built-in stove or refrigerator.

Open-end mortgage. At the discretion of the lender, during the term of the loan the borrower may at a later date borrow again, up to the amount of the original loan, and in certain cases more. The interest rate for new loans will reflect the current market charges.

Second mortgage (or trust deed). If the down payment is more than you have available or wish to pay, it is sometimes possible to get the difference from the previous owner or another lender.

A second mortgage or trust deed means the borrower carries a tremendous burden for amortization, as the loan is usually short term. The interest rate is usually higher than that for the first mortgage, and you frequently have a balloon payment at the end of the three-, five- or ten-year term. Can you afford all this? You may be better off finding a house you can carry without the extra load.

and house requirements that will qualify you for a mortgage.

Never buy property unseen. People have bought Florida land that lies under water and southwestern property called a"desert paradise"that is desert, but a far cry from paradise.

When you build, get the guidance of an architect who knows your family's needs and likes. He can help you understand blueprints and visualize the size and arrangement of rooms. Then you can make changes in the plans, inexpensively, before building starts. Later changes cost more.

Your contract with the builder should specify every material to be used in the construction, plus the landscaping and inside decorating he will do. You can often lower the cost by arranging to do landscaping and inside decorating yourself.

A prefabricated house—partly manufactured elsewhere and put together on your land—costs far less than one built entirely from scratch. The contractor charges for his labor and materials. Again, you can save some of these labor costs if you arrange to do some jobs yourself. But be sure you have the ability to handle them and that your lender is agreeable.

Ways to Cut
Operating Costs in
Cold Weather Areas

You'll lower your heating costs if you invest in storm windows, at least for the cold (usually the north) sides of the house. Remember that heat does escape through ordinary glass windows even when they are kept closed. Storm windows also help to prevent cracks in paint surfaces caused by extreme weather contrasts.

Plan to hire local boys to rake and stack leaves in the fall and to shovel snow in winter.

Before you invest in a snowplow, chat with your neighbors to explore renting or buying one as a group, sharing the use and the cost.

Avoid unnecessary moves

When you need more space for family needs, or want it because your family has become more affluent, consider ways of expanding your present house before you move. An expansion attic is ideal for another bedroom, for example, and a building expert can tell you whether zoning will permit it and if the foundation and structure of the house are strong enough to carry the extra load. Can you turn a porch into another bedroom? Divide a room? Move a wall outward?

Ask local builders to look at your house and suggest ways and costs. Judge these against the cost of moving, which can involve bills for paints and wallpapers, curtains, some rugs and furniture and the mover's charge. Frequently you can finance the extras you want through an addition to your existing loan or a new property improvement loan at a savings and loan association.

Consider a cooperative or condominium

If you plan to live in an apartment, compare the annual cost of comparable space in a cooperative or condominium.

A co-op "owner" is actually a stockholder in the entire building; the stock ownership gives him the right to live in one of the apartments. The size and desirability of the apartment determine the value of stock you own. You pay a proportionate share—called monthly maintenance—toward the building's overhead and are responsible for your own apartment's repairs, alteration, upkeep and appliance replacement.

You can take income tax deductions for your share of the building's real estate taxes, and your share of its mortgage interest. Those income tax deductions mean, in effect, much lower annual costs for your housing compared with renting.

In a few cases, when you sell a co-op you must have the approval of the other stockholders or may have to offer it back to the corporation at the original price. So look into the building's rules and regulations.

With older co-op buildings, it's a good idea to chat with other owners or neighbors, if possible, about the condition of the house. You should also ask the real estate agent. If major repairs or replacements are imminent, your monthly maintenance charges might have to go up to pay these bills.

When you buy a condominium you take title to the apartment itself, and have an interest in joint facilities, rather than buying stock in the building. In some states you have the freedom to negotiate your own mortgage terms; you own real estate that is salable on the open market at a possible profit; you do not shoulder the cost of taxes and mortgage interest for empty apartments. However, the situation varies in different states, so know your local market well before you go ahead.

As a condominium owner you do have costs for amortization and interest on any mortgage you acquired to buy the apartment, but you are building up an equity. You have a monthly maintenance charge for the joint facilities (heat, roof repair, hallway cleaning and lighting, etc.) and you pay for your own decoration, repairs and appliances. You also pay real estate taxes on your individual apartment. You get all the Federal income tax advantages that a homeowner can claim.

Don't rush to remodel

It's exciting to remodel a house and adapt it to your own personality and needs. But don't rush to remodel it before, or as soon as, you move in. Consider living in it for at least a year to see how it works. You might save a lot of money this way. There will be happy surprises—structural quirks can lend charm to a house once you get used to them, room arrangements that worried you at first often prove to "live" beautifully after a while.

The year will give you a chance to learn what really should be changed to improve your family's living. Then, too, by waiting before you remodel you will have time to get comparative bids from several sources, find ways to do some of the work yourself and shop around to get good buys in materials.

Do it yourself

The biggest dollar-saver in running or remodeling a house is a husband who is handy. There are plenty of how-to books and manuals to help him, and manufacturers of materials are glad to give advice and free instruction brochures.

In one family, for example, the husband built a small back porch himself and put a shower-type rod all around it. The wife bought canvas awning fabric and made café-type drapes to hang from them, shading the porch from the sun. The whole porch cost little, but a contractor had asked $500 for a comparable job.

Women can be "handymen," too. A recent study indicated that wives are actually better at certain jobs—refinishing and painting, for example—than husbands. Try steaming off old wallpaper yourself, using rented machines or wipe-on preparations that help force water through the paper into the old paste. You can even rent floor scraping equipment from hardware or home machinery rental stores.

Let your neighbor help

Exchanging skills with a neighbor is another dollar-stretching trick. In one family, for example, the husband is an accountant and his neighbor is skilled as a plumber. The neighbor does plumbing emergency and replacement jobs for both families and the accountant prepares the neighbor's income tax returns.

Consider, too, the possibility of buying or renting power tools, electric mower and extension ladder as a neighborhood group. You can all use them and share the cost.

Save when you buy services

Some husbands don't like or can't do household repairs or maintenance chores. A man unaccustomed to crawling over a rooftop to clean gutters or fix shingles does expose himself to dangerous and expensive accidents and probably won't do the best possible job, either. You will do better to hire outside help and get the most for your dollar.

Local boys often charge very little for lawn work. If the boys don't come ringing your bell to ask for work, check friends and neighbors to find them.

Many high schools and colleges run employment centers to help students earn money. They will send you eager, hard-working boys to mow grass, move furniture, hose down the garage and do countless other jobs.

"Moonlighters" can save you money, too. In almost every community there are skilled workmen who work evenings, holidays and weekends for comparatively little cost. Moon-lighters are generally known to one another. A plumber may be able to recommend a good man to repair your driveway or build cement steps. It pays to ask.

Save when you paint

Painters and paperhangers tend to be busiest before holi-days and in the autumn. Ask how you might save money if you arrange for the work to be done in an off-season. The cost of labor is the major part of the expense, so insist that the painter buy the best paints, or you supply them yourself.

The most important part of a paint job is proper prep-aration of the surfaces. They should be thoroughly cleaned and patched before a new coat is applied. Make sure doors and windows are planed so they close properly before the paint-ing. Have hardware removed, not painted over : several coats of paint over hardware can ruin the closing of doors and win-dows, which will lower the value of the house.

Use skilled workmen and reliable sources

In any home service, unreliable and inept people are costly to you, as well as troublesome to deal with. It's worth your time to get recommendations from people whose judg-ment you respect and who have used the worker. Go to see the jobs that have been completed in other homes if you can.

Be suspicious of any company that promises to use the job it does on your house as a model, and to give you commis-sions. This often costs as much, if not more, than a local contractor would charge, and is apt to be second-rate. If the company actually does get other jobs by using your house as a model, chances are slim that you'll ever be informed about it.

Watch out for itinerants who display bogus identification cards and introduce themselves as furnace inspectors. They will dismantle your furnace, announce that the whole works is about to blow apart and advise you to sign a contract for an extensive and expensive overhaul. Your furnace may actually be in A-1 condition, so be sure to check it out with a local, reliable expert.

Bell ringers who offer free termite inspection will probably emerge from your cellar or crawl space with a foreboding look and pronouncement that the area or entire house is badly infested. Even it it is true, you'll do better to contract for termite control with a local firm that depends on neighborhood goodwill.

Lower your heating costs

Heating engineers argue among themselves over whether or not you save money by turning down the thermostat at night and during the day when no one is home. Some say that turning heat down saves from $50 to $100 a year. Others maintain that the fuel needed to bring up the heat and warm a cold house costs at least that or even more.

But you undeniably save fuel costs in cold weather if you close doors between rooms. Pull the window shades and close the blinds, shutters and curtains in rooms you don't use.

Compare the costs of oil, gas and electricity in your particular area before installing a heating hystem. But consider, too, how much of each of the three you use in running other systems in your house. For the more you use of any single utility, the lower your "unit" cost will be. If your heat bills seem unduly high, consider changing your fuel.

Good insulation can cut fuel costs from $75 to $150 a year. You may be able to install it yourself in your attic—the most important area. Ask dealers of insulation materials for advice.

Avoid termite trouble

Don't worry unduly about termites, but always have a termite inspection before you buy a house. If your inspection uncovers any infestation or damage, the former owner should repair it or lower his price to cover the repair cost.

You can have a house inspected for termites once a year. Termite-proof immediately at any sign of trouble. Some exterminators give a five-year guarantee and offer an additional insurance plan for a nominal sum afterward.

Don't go down the garden path

You will save yourself money and a lot of edging and weeding if you keep your flowering plots small. Place them artfully for dramatic effect and pick your flowers for their vivid colors. Stick to the sturdy kinds.

The perennials give a wonderful permanent garden and are inexpensive because they come up year after year. If you want annuals, buy them in flats, 100 to a flat, at little cost.

Patronize your local nurseryman. At first he may seem to be more expensive than roadstands or sales you read about. But he is familiar with your area and can advise you on the shrubs, bushes and flowers that adapt well to your soil. Stay away from itinerants who offer humus and plantings from trucks—these are often inferior in quality.

If you rent a house

Renting does not give you the equity-building advantages of home owning. But to make economic sense you should not buy a house unless you expect to live in it for at least five years, to amortize the closing costs. If you plan to live in it less time than that, the cost of buying is too high and you will be better off to rent.

When you do rent, know your rights and responsibilities, for as with everything else, mistakes are costly.

Be sure your lease clearly states what you are responsible for and what you get from the owner. Who pays for landscaping? For decorating? If the owner is responsible for decorating, what does it include? What rights do you have? For example, can you change the paint colors or wallpaper as you wish?

Who pays for repairs and maintenance? For plumbing? If the owner pays, try to get written permission to call in a plumber or electrician of the owner's choosing should the need arise. Some owners tinker before calling an expert, to your great inconvenience. If you can call a serviceman directly, you can have the work done quickly, and done right, because *you* will be doing the supervising.

Heat is always the tenant's responsibility in a one-family house, so find out how much it totaled last year. Check the local utility company on its rates. Gas and electricity will be your responsibility, too. If you pay for water, get the rates from the local water company, as well as last year's bill for the house.

If there are no sewers, ask about the construction of the drain field and the size of the septic tanks. How often is it necessary to clean the system and how much does it cost? You may have to pay the costs for keeping it clean.

If there is no municipal rubbish collection, how much will cartage cost you each month?

Renting an apartment

When you seek to rent an apartment, comb the neighborhoods you like to find "Vacancy" and "For Rent" signs. Study the newspaper real estate classified ads. It's a good idea to ask neighborhood tradesmen and your friends whether anyone they know is moving, and the superintendents of buildings you like about chances of vacancies coming up.

A good real estate broker can also help. He knows the buildings that are vacant, and the advantages of different neighborhoods, buildings and apartments.

Read that apartment lease

Leases usually give landlords at least a month's rent money as security, without interest to you and returnable only when you leave the apartment. This payment protects the landlord against damage to his property through carelessness and against your falling behind in rent or absconding.

The lease should protect you, too. Make sure everything that the landlord promises orally is put down in writing. Is he responsible for repairs of broken windows, screens, and for all the appliances that come with the apartment, including air conditioners? If gas and electricity are included in the rent, the lease should say so.

Does the lease list all the equipment that comes with the apartment? Usually this means refrigerator, stove, lighting fixtures, air conditioning units and window blinds. If other appliances are in the apartment, the lease should guarantee that they will remain, if you want them, or will be removed by the landlord if you don't want them. Otherwise you will have to pay for having them disconnected and stored. Does the lease give a decorating timetable, stating whether the landlord does the painting and how often?

Does it specify building services—a round-the-clock attendant, for example?

Are pets allowed? You may not have even a goldfish now, but the day might come when you'll want a dog or cat.

Must you put down carpeting? Some leases say that a tenant must carpet as much as 90 percent of his apartment if the downstairs neighbors complain of noise.

Does the lease give you permission to sublet if you want to move?

Does it state how many persons may occupy the apartment? If so, does the figure allow for children or friends and relatives who may join your household? Landlords have demanded and received a rent increase when a tenant's family grew.

When you move

Select your moving company at least several weeks in advance, checking the reputation of its agents in both your old and new locations. If a company has no agent near your new address, it will be difficult to settle any problems that might arise during the move.

Insist that the company send a representative to your home to see exactly what and how much you want to move. You have a legal right to this visit, and it is the only way you can get an accurate estimate of your moving costs.

With interstate moves you pay by the weight, mileage and extra services and all rates are pretty much the same. But if you are moving within your state you may benefit from some price competition. Get estimates from at least two or three companies and observe how conscientiously they estimate and price the various elements of their service.

Tricks to lower costs

If you have a choice, avoid moving in the summer, when almost two-thirds of all moves take place. You may be able to get a better price when business slacks off, and you'll undoubtedly get better service, meaning fewer headaches and losses for you.

For long-distance moves, allow yourself several days leeway at both ends so you can avoid emergency charges. For example, if the van arrives late to pick up, you might have to pay extra rent in your old place. If the mover delivers to your new home ahead of schedule, there is a chance of storage charges unless the truck can unload on arrival.

Prepare traveler's checks to pay immediately if you contract for a C.O.D. move. You are expected to pay the driver the entire bill before your furniture comes off the van. If you can't do it within a few hours, he can charge extra for each hour he waits between 8 A.M. and 5 P.M. He can also legally store your furniture, which will cost you a full month's storage plus other extra charges.

Instead of moving C.O.D., try to get a 30-day credit agreement—in writing—to avoid the whole problem. This deferred payment plan also gives you more bargaining power with the company in case of trouble. But don't agree to an installment plan financed by a loan company, which will give you no arguing power at all.

Before the move, throw out or give away whatever you won't use in your new home. Don't buy packing cartons from the mover when you can get them free from supermarkets, furniture and liquor stores. Find out how to pack your own books, dishes, decorations and kitchen items; padding with plenty of newspaper helps to prevent breakage. If the movers pack for you (remember that you are entitled to unpacking, too, for the price) don't let them leave containers half full. You are paying for each container used.

Tag the furniture and containers for the rooms they go into in the new house. Ask the movers to put furniture in the position you think will be permanent or close to it. Your moving charge includes one placement. It will cost you money and bother to reposition heavy furniture later.

Protect yourself

Keep a list of everying loaded on the van. Watch the driver's notations of the condition of items on his inventory sheet to make sure his description fits the facts, in case you have to make a claim.

It's a good idea to take out your own insurance against loss or damage before the move, as the mover's insurance does not protect you adequately and the small one-time premium will usually be less than the value of any claim you need to make.

When the move has been completed, check your possessions against the list you made before, and ask the driver to sign for broken or missing articles on the itemized and receipted bill which you keep. Don't sign his inventory sheet without writing down any damage or loss that you spot. Also state that this is not final, as hidden losses and damage may emerge later.

You should have nine months to file a claim or add to it. If you don't get satisfactory response, go to the mover's insurance company, and write to the Director, Bureau of Operations, Interstate Commerce Commission, Washington, D.C., which can help expedite a quicker settlement.

POINTS TO REMEMBER

1. Choose a house that is inexpensive to maintain. Use a checklist to compare factors such as taxes, heating, water, repairs, decorating, gardening, etc.

2. Negotiate the price coolly. Offer less than the seller asks and proceed from there. Put down as much cash as you can. Take out as small a mortgage as practical and pay it back quickly to save total dollar costs on the financing.

3. Before buying or building, evaluate the area in terms of schools, churches, shopping and accessibility. Good community services help maintain the price of the house later when *you* want to sell.

4. Consult an architect before you build a house. Do remodeling and repairs yourself whenever possible. When you can't, use skilled workmen. You save money by hiring moonlighters, high school students for routine chores, and by exchanging skills with neighbors and friends.

5. Before renting an apartment, compare the cost of comparable space in a co-op or condominium. Owning may cost less than renting because of the income tax benefits you get.

Chapter Eight

MORE SAVINGS

The same kind of know-how that enables anyone to stretch dollars for the basic family needs—food, clothing, shelter and so on—will get you more for your money in other kinds of spending necessary in our complex society. For example, most families require life and medical insurance.

Dont "save" within your life insurance

It may sound great to build up a "cash value" that is yours to keep when you outlive an insurance plan. But if you have to drop the plan because you can't keep up the high premiums, you will have the costs of buying new insurance—or find yourself without protection at the very moment when you need it.

If the high premiums for the savings in the "ordinary" or "straight" life plans force you to buy less insurance than your family needs, should the breadwinner die, you have cheated yourself out of the first thing insurance is supposed to provide: protection. When you are dollar-stretching, term insurance is your best buy.

To plan your own insurance needs, talk with three different brokers you might like to work with. Ask each to prepare a full insurance program for you. You will learn a lot from how each approaches your problem and shows concern for your welfare. You can tell them you are comparing plans. Good brokers should be willing to compete for your business.

Each will give your needs more careful thought and work harder to save your money.

Don't buy more, or less, insurance than you need. A rule of thumb states that the face value of life insurance should be four or five times your annual income. Like most rules, it doesn't always apply to individual cases. The Institute of Life Insurance has worked out a more reliable formula for planning family needs. It goes:

$$\textbf{CRE } \tfrac{1}{2} \; \tfrac{1}{4} \; \tfrac{1}{2}$$

"C" stands for the amount of immediate cash needed if a husband dies. Plan as if it were to happen tomorrow. Of course you hope it won't, but base your planning realistically on that assumption. Immediately you would need: cash for hospital fees, funeral expenses, debts, perhaps inheritance taxes and executor's fees.

Social Security will provide up to $255 for such needs and most veterans are eligible for an additional $250. Get a schedule of payments for your income level by writing the Social Security Administration.

You can figure on using savings accounts and stocks and bonds—your liquid assets—to help meet immediate expenses. Often mortgage life insurance can protect your home investment. Life insurance will cover whatever is not met in some other way. But it has to do more:

"R" in that formula stands for readjustment money. Time is needed to decide whether to sell the house or the car, and whether the mother should get a job. She may need a refresher course or some kind of training. There should be enough money—income for a year or two—to make these decisions wisely, without rushing into something to be regretted later. When a house must be sold, for example, you want time to get a good price.

"E" stands for educational funds for the children. Even when children are very young and have no idea whether they want to go to college, you should provide for them in case they do. College now costs between $2,000 and $4,000 a year and the cost is going up. The children may be able to get scholarships or loans, but the chances are they'll need additional help, even if they plan to work part-time. A college education savings fund, started early and added to regularly, is the most profitable way to build up the amounts they will need, because of the good interest earnings. Life insurance can also be used to meet this need.

The "½" stands for income for your family during the children's growing years. It refers to half of the husband's present monthly earnings according to one rule of thumb that a family can live three-quarters as well on half the husband's income after his death.

Social Security offsets some expenses during this period, but not all. The rest comes from life insurance payments.

The "¼" stands for lifetime income for the widow on the premise that she will need at least one-quarter of her husband's monthly salary after the children have left home. Social Security payments stop when the youngest child reaches 18, unless he or she is in school or college, when they continue to age 22. Payments resume when the widow is 60 or 62, but on a reduced basis. Do your arithmetic to come up with how much you'll need at today's prices.

The final "½" stands for retirement income. The odds are, after all, that both husband and wife will live well beyond retirement age, and some experts calculate that half the husband's monthly income, plus Social Security and perhaps a company retirement fund, will meet a retired couple's income needs.

But again, remember that this item can go when children are young and a dollar-stretching budget has to provide adequate insurance for them.

Review your insurance program at least once every five years to make sure it keeps pace with your family's standard of living and rising costs. Whenever a child is born, it affects your needs.

Once you figure out how much insurance you need, you

have to select the *type* of policy. Basically there are two types: term and permanent.

GI insurance, available to anyone who has served in the Armed Forces, is term insurance and the cheapest and best kind. Buy all you are allowed. A unique benefit is the cancellation of premiums, while the death payment stays in force if the policyholder should become totally and permanently disabled.

Group term life insurance may be available where you work or through any organization you belong to. It always represents a savings because there is no salesman's commission to pay.

The most common forms of term insurance are five-year renewable and decreasing term. Five-year renewable term insurance pays a fixed death benefit and is renewable every five years, at an increased premium because of the older age of the insured person.

Decreasing term insurance offers a death payment that decreases every year, while the premiums stay the same. At the beginning, when children are very young, you get more insurance per premium dollar with this type. Later it may be converted to permanent "ordinary" or "straight" life insurance.

The two basic forms of permanent insurance are straight life and endowment.

In the first, the policyholder pays a fixed premium—for a fixed death benefit—which is payable as long as he lives.

While the policyholder is alive, it may be cashed in for some specified amount. This is called cash surrender value. When anyone borrows against life insurance, the cash surrender value is the sum that serves as collateral.

Endowment insurance is similar to straight life except that after a given number of years, or at a given age, such as 65, the full value is paid to the policyholder. If he dies prematurely, the full value is paid to the beneficiary. Many people use this to accumulate a given sum of money by a specified time.

Permanent insurance is more expensive than term because of its extra benefits. Insurance that pays retirement benefits is the most expensive of all.

Some insurance salesmen try to sell life insurance for children. Remember that life insurance is for the protection of income. Why pay premiums on a child?

If the wife works and the family's standard of living depends on it, she should be covered. Many experts now believe that her work in the home and caring for children is also worth money. Her duties would have to be taken over by a housekeeper and other outside services, at least until the husband remarries. A small insurance program should protect the family in that event.

Take out medical insurance

Medical insurance is more necessary than ever as doctor's fees and hospital charges soar. They are already way beyond the average family's ability to pay out of income.

Many companies enroll employees in Blue Cross and/or Blue Shield programs to cover hospital and surgical bills. Many also offer major medical insurance plans and employees may enroll the whole family. Modest deductions are made from paychecks to pay premiums. You always save by applying for the coverage as a member of a group.

If your employer does not offer these, find out if some organization you belong to does, or propose that it set up such a plan. If none of these are possible, take out some—at least Blue Cross—on your own.

Workmen's Compensation laws provide payments to employees who are injured or become ill as a result of their work. The compensations vary from state to state. Employers are required to post a notice about them; read it; know what you are entitled to get.

Disability insurance, giving you at least some income during a long recuperation from an accident or illness, also may be provided by your employer or union or may be available as part of your life insurance policy. You may not need further coverage. But know the details of your present coverage so that you can provide for yourself if it is inadequate. In that case take out a separate policy. It is generally inexpensive.

Often insurance has deductible clauses. A $100 deductible clause, for example, means you pay the first $100, and the insurance pays the rest. Always have ready funds, in savings, to meet that amount.

Whenever you take out insurance, through a group or on your own, read the policy thoroughly to know when and how to file a claim. Keep records of all doctor and drug bills to verify your claims.

When you borrow money

Money, as everything else, costs less at some places than at others. A loan from a thrift institution is generally cheapest. Finance company loans are the most expensive, because they take greater risks. The loan company should be the last resort of the borrower and used only for an absolute necessity. Always investigate the cost of a loan at a savings and loan institution—especially when it is for a house —or at a bank, before you go to a finance company.

For most types of loans from savings institutions you do not need to have an account there to borrow money. You do have to measure up to the three C's—Character, Capacity (to repay) and Collateral. A savings institution wants to know whether you're reliable; whether, on your income, you can afford to borrow the amount you want; and whether you have any stocks or bonds to present as collateral—assurance that you will repay the loan. You may be able to borrow 20 or 30 percent of your annual gross income, depending on the institution.

As an individual you can get an auto, personal or other loan on an installment plan, paying back a specified amount each month over a predetermined period: most personal loans are for two years, most auto loans for three.

There also are time loans secured by collateral and repayable over a three- or six-month period. You may be able to borrow the cash surrender value of your life insurance policy, or 70 percent of the market value of the stocks or bonds you put up for collateral. You can repay a loan in a lump sum, saving money on interest charges.

Interest rates vary—among banks and from year to year, as well as by the type of loan you secure. If you can wait, don't borrow when credit is tight. Do your own arithmetic to see how much any bank rate actually costs you, and comparison-shop among banks as you would for any other service.

Under the national Truth-in-Lending Act, all institutions that lend money to consumers must tell how much the interest will be on a yearly basis. A one percent interest charge per month, for example, is 12 percent per year, and 1½ percent monthly is 18 percent annually. The true cost of "discounted" rates, usually twice the percentage of the discounted figure, must be given. This new law simplifies your comparison-shopping.

Passbook loans are usually the most economical loans of all. If you have a savings account in a savings and loan association or bank, you can borrow against it. Your savings account stays intact with the lender, earning money as always. Again, shop among savings institutions. For example, at one savings and loan association, if you will be earning 5 percent on your savings, and your loan costs 6 percent, the actual cost of the loan to you is only 1 percent.

Try a credit union

Many companies, churches, fraternal organizations and the like have credit unions—a sort of savings and loan co-operative. The members agree to save among themselves and lend to one another. They build up a fund by buying shares worth $5 each in the credit union.

The law permits credit union loans on only your signature up to $750, and collateral loans in larger amounts. You repay weekly, semimonthly or monthly. The top interest rate is one percent per month on the unpaid balance, which must include all charges. Many credit unions charge less—some as little as half of one percent.

For example, on a federally chartered credit union loan of $100, repaid in equal monthly installments, the total cost at the top interest rate is:

$5.50 for 10 months	$10.50 for 20 months
$6.50 for 12 months	$12.50 for 24 months

Federal credit unions are not insured by the Federal government or any Federal agency.

Stay away from revolving accounts

The revolving charge accounts offered by most department stores are intended for big purchases. You agree to pay a certain amount each month and are charged interest on the balance. But often there is a carrying charge as well. This isn't interest, but it costs you money and must be calculated as part of your total price. Don't use revolving accounts to buying clothing and other small items.

Wherever you borrow, there are penalties for failure to meet payments. The failure also may jeopardize your ability to borrow in the future.

How to save on drugs

Discount drug stores sell both prescription and non-prescription medicines at ten to 25 percent less than regular drugstores. Shop around or inquire among friends to find one. Buy as many other items as you can while you are in the store, since the same discounts are applied to toothpaste, shampoo, facial tissue, etc. Also find out about the discount drug companies that offer their own private brands of vitamins, mouthwashes and cream rinses. The medicines must meet the same Federal requirements as do national brands.

Why not order drugs from big discounters by mail? Not prescription drugs that you need right away but staples such as vitamins. Check the prices in the discount company's brochure against the ones in your local discount store to see how they compare before you mail out your order.

Whenever your doctor writes you a prescription, ask him to specify the *generic* name of the medicine rather than the brand name. Remember: you pay for the advertising and the prestige of the drugs sold under brand names by big pharmaceutical manufacturers. They often contain the same ingredients as drugs sold under generic names by companies that do not advertise, but generic-name drugs cost much less.

Dollar-stretch the children's education

More and more careers require a college education these days. There is no need to let children miss out on college when so many scholarship and loan programs make up for what parents cannot pay out of income.

A college education doesn't require an expensive Ivy League or even a private college. Boarding adds nothing to its value. State universities are less expensive than private colleges, and if there is a state university or extension near you, your son or daughter can go to classes there and live at home.

College students can also take part-time jobs, such as waiting on tables or operating a switchboard, and summer jobs to work their way through college.

High school students who foresee the need for financial assistance should take the National Merit Scholarship Test in their junior year. Even if they do not get a National Merit Scholarship, they will interest colleges in helping them through some other kind of grant or loan, if they do well on the test.

Many large companies offer scholarships, or partial scholarships, to children of employees. If you are choosing among several jobs, it could be worth your while to find out whether the companies involved have such a fringe benefit —it could be worth thousands of dollars to you.

Colleges and universities offer both scholarships and

loans, depending on need and scholastic ability. Information about them is included in the college catalogue. But find out about scholastic requirements from your high school dean or guidance office when your child begins high school.

A student applies for financial assistance when he makes his college application. In his senior high school year, parents submit a confidential statement through the high school, disclosing income and other financial responsibilities. A request for aid does not prejudice a student's admission chances.

Your own community may also have scholarship programs for children of your area. The high school dean or guidance office can direct you to the sources. Call for an appointment and talk over your family situation candidly.

Educational loans of all types—whether from colleges, community organizations or from savings and loan associations and banks—are more favorable to the borrower than most. Usually they defer payment until some time after the student has graduated, and have reduced interest charges. Look for "incentive" loans. For example, some community and professional-association loans are interest-free. Some organizations cancel a portion of the loan if the student agrees to spend a period of time after graduation in specified work—teaching, perhaps.

High school deans, principals and guidance offices are the best source of more detailed information.

Save on vacations

You don't have to take your vacation when everyone else goes, when prices are highest and the crowds biggest. Go out of season, when airlines, resorts and hotels drop their rates to attract you. Explore the tourist attractions in your own state. If you hanker to see faraway states, save travel costs by using your own car or traveling by the new air-conditioned and comfortable buses. Ask about tour plans.

Camping trips, with tents, sleeping bags and portable

gas stove, are becoming popular in the U.S. because they offer a complete change, are amazingly inexpensive, relaxing and can be done almost everywhere in the country. You stay in state or national parks that are well designed for camping facilities—boating, fishing, hunting, climbing, sightseeing and more. You can rent tents and camping equipment, even trailers.

If this is your year to see Europe, go to the less expensive countries (Ireland, the Netherlands, Portugal, Spain). See Europe in winter and South America in summer. To cut the cost of air fare: travel between Mondays and Thursdays; go with a group in a chartered plane; buy a 21-day excursion ticket; always ask about family plans and about the new Group Inclusive Tour air fares.

Don't invest in special "travel" clothing. Items from your regular wardrobe will be entirely suitable. Plan to clean things en route, and travel light.

Save on liquor, cigarettes, records, magazines

You can find surprisingly big liquor savings when you buy private labels. The famous distillers don't want to lower their prices but do want to lower their overhead by selling more, so they sell in bulk to individual dealers. These apply their own label and sell to you at reduced prices—sometimes only half the amount of a comparable famous brand liquor. A study showed, for example, that a fifth of liquor with an obscure label, costing $3.98, was as good as and amazingly like a fifth bottle carrying a well-known trade name that cost $8.95. The cost difference—more than 100 percent.

Cigarettes are cheaper by the carton, liquor by the case (find a store that will make up a case of different kinds of liquor) and paint by the gallon—if you can afford the initial outlay and only if you are able to use all you buy.

Buy records in discount houses, either in the department of a big store or in a place that specializes in records. The biggest savings in records, however, are now in many public libraries, where you can borrow them free. Records not immediately available can be reserved for only a couple of pennies.

Some libraries check out magazines, too. But when you buy a magazine, remember that it costs less by subscription than on the newsstand, and magazines make special low offers to new subscribers—usually in an advertising insert in the magazine or in the mail.

Dine out less expensively

Eating in a restaurant is always a lot more expensive than eating at home. If you're going out to the movies or theater with friends, why not have dinner at your home and go out after? Next time arrange to eat at their house. Or have dinner at home separately, see the movie and then visit over a late snack.

If you must have dinner out, plan to enjoy cocktails at home. At the restaurant, order only the main dish and coffee from the à la carte menu. You are cutting out only the fattening frills like appetizer, soup and dessert. When you add the total bill, it includes taxes and there is no reason to figure them in order to calculate 20 percent for a tip.

Avoid the high-fashion restaurants and the tourist spots. Chinese restaurants are well known for delicious food served in large portions for little money. Many other ethnic restaurants—Armenian and Indian, for example—offer similar bargains and an unusual treat. Ironically, sometimes older or apartment-hotel restaurants offer excellent meals at moderate prices—and don't have waiting lines.

Save movie money

Avoid first-run houses; the same films cost less in your neighborhood. It's just as smart to wait until they are bought for television, too—movies only two years old are now being shown on TV. See them for nothing.

Film festivals of famous old movies often come to local theaters; they may be the best entertainment buy available. If your museum has film programs, you'll see the movie classics, and museums charge only a dollar or so for admission.

Take control of your "contributions"

Some "charities" are not only undeserving—they are outright frauds that prey on your response to strong emotional appeals. You should do your giving on a planned basis, deciding when you make your yearly budget just how much you will give.

There are more good causes than you can help and you have the right and duty to pick the ones that are meaningful to you. If you don't know which they are now, get a list of approved charities from the Internal Revenue Service, which allows you to deduct the donations from your tax. Choose your contributions as carefully as any other expenditure. Be firm about saying no to the others, no matter how worthy.

POINTS TO REMEMBER

1. Insurance is meant to provide protection in case of death, not savings. When you're dollar-stretching, term insurance is your best buy.

2. Borrowing costs money, but a loan from a thrift institution is usually the cheapest.

3. For your children's education, take advantage of state universities, scholarships and special grants. Educational loans are generally more favorable to the borrower than other loans.

4. Save on liquor bills by buying a private label that costs about half as much as a famous name brand—they are frequently the same quality. Buy by the case. Borrow records from libraries.

5. When dining out, avoid high-fashion restaurants (cut bills by having cocktails at home). Wait for films to be shown at your neighborhood movie house. Wait longer, and you can see them for nothing—on TV. Also, see movies in museums.

Chapter Nine

WHAT DO YOU DO WITH MONEY YOU SAVE?

Smart dollar-stretching gives you money you can regard as surplus, over and above your normal needs for living.

This presents a problem.

The extra dollars must be put to work earning more extra dollars for you, but there are many ways to put money to work. Some are suitable for the average American family; others require more financial know-how than most families have. We will discuss several ways of putting your dollars to work. Then you can determine which way, or combination of ways, is most suitable for your particular situation.

Investments

Among the investment avenues open to the average family are stocks, bonds, government securities and real estate. These investments may be used singly or in combination, but they are not "do-it-yourself" projects. All require the use of professional help.

Let's consider stocks first, because of all investment avenues they capture the imagination of most people. There is no question that stocks you buy may go up in value; it is also true that they can decrease in value.

In buying stocks you have to make up your mind on the approach you want to take. You can buy a speculative growth stock that you hope will increase dramatically in price, but these stocks normally pay only a modest dividend, if any. On the other hand, you can buy a blue chip stock that normally will not fluctuate very much in price—but that does pay a relatively good dividend rate. Some blue chip stocks pay as much as 5 percent, but these are rare and the more common rate now would be 3 to 4 percent.

Frankly, stocks are an investment to be pursued only after you have set up a satisfactory savings program, a program which will provide you with extra funds that are also earning good dividends. Even then, seek help from a stockbroker who will at least be able to help you avoid most of the numerous pitfalls.

Much of the financial know-how you need for the stock market is also helpful in the bond market. Bonds are fixed income investments; they do not fluctuate in value as stocks do. Bonds are issued by large corporations, by municipalities, by the United States government and many of its agencies.

The rate of return on bonds is generally very conservative. However, in certain situations in the economy, such as a period of very tight money, bond rates become more attractive.

Another interesting feature about bonds is that when they are issued by municipalities—cities, towns, counties, etc. —they are tax-exempt.

Under normal circumstances, municipal bonds would only be of interest to families in higher tax brackets. Here again, however, since municipal bonds vary in type and in worth, you should avoid purchasing them without advice from your bond broker.

Government securities can certainly be classed as a triple-A investment. They are as secure as the government itself. But the rate of return is usually lower than other market investments.

For example, most of us are familiar with the smaller kind of government securities such as Series H, F and G bonds. A good example of this type were the bonds issued during World War II to finance the nation's war efforts. You could buy one of these bonds for $18.75 and at maturity, ten years later, you would collect $25.00—secure but hardly a princely rate of return.

From the foregoing it is easy to see that, in general, government bonds are not intended for the average family's investment. The government bond market is used in most cases by large investors—financial institutions, insurance companies, large corporations—for tax advantages and to fulfill legal investment requirements.

Another popular investment is real estate. Here again, there are a lot of "caution-go-slow" signs along the way. When most people talk of real estate investments they refer in the main to rental properties. For many families a real estate investment might take the shape of buying a two-unit apartment building, living on one floor and renting out the other one.

Investing in real estate also requires know-how and is not recommended for the amateur. You must give careful thought to how much it will cost you to maintain it. In this way you will be able to set your rental schedule so that you reap a reasonable profit on your investment.

But—and this is a big but—there is one avenue of real estate investment that is recommended for most American families—a home of your own. Your own home will most likely be the largest single investment you will ever make in your life. It will also be the most rewarding one. Here's why:

Personal security. The comfortable feeling that comes with possession.

Stability. Nobody but you has the right to say whether you'll remain in the house or move.

Investment. You're getting something tangible for your money. At the end of ten years, an owner has acquired a large equity in his property. A tenant over the same period can only show worthless receipts for his rent money. Someday the house will be completely yours and may pay a handsome return on your invested money.

Independence. It's your own property, and you can do what you like with it within legal limitations.

Roots. Since most homeowners intend to live in their homes a long time, they usually take an active part in the civic affairs of the community. This is particularly important if you have children.

Status. Owning your home as a rule improves your credit standing.

Protection. Your home is a safeguard against inflation. In prosperous times, real estate increases in value.

Tax advantage. You can deduct the interest you pay on the mortgage, and the taxes you pay on your home, on your income tax return.

Why is home ownership becoming ever more popular? According to the last census, taken in 1960, some 62 percent— a majority—of American families have chosen to buy homes. One important explanation has to do with dollars and cents. When you rent you have one big cost that you *don't* have when you buy. Analyze your rent payment, and you will find that the money you give your landlord covers the following:

1. The original cost of the house.
2. The cost of financing the house.
3. Upkeep, rehabilitation and repairs.
4. Taxes and insurance.
5. A profit to the landlord.

Now analyze the costs of home ownership. You'll find they cover the following:

1. The original cost of the house.
2. The cost of financing the house.
3. Upkeep, rehabilitation and repairs.
4. Taxes and insurance.

What's missing from the cost of home ownership? Why, "profit to the landlord," of course. Often renters overlook this aspect of their rent payment. Yet they know that the landlord has invested his money in the house and that he has done so because he expects a return—a profit—on the investment.

When you buy, it is not primarily to make a profit. You buy for the basic purpose of acquiring adequate shelter.

Also, as we have seen, when you own a house you deduct your taxes and the interest on your mortgage from your income tax. You have to pay the landlord for these, but you cannot deduct them.

Experts have deeply probed the question of how much the average family can spend for housing, either for rent or for home ownership. They have made two findings which have been widely accepted as general guides to the family planning home ownership. One of them is that you can afford roughly one week's take-home pay out of each month's salary for housing expenses. The other is that the cost of the home should not be more than two and one half times the family's annual take-home income.

Obviously families, like individuals, have different tastes, habits and preferences. Some spend more on recreation than others and cannot spend as much as one week of monthly income for housing. Some have more children than others and must budget more for food, clothing and medical care—and less for housing. Some families can allot more than a week out of a month's income for housing because they have larger incomes and prefer to use their homes for entertainment and for recreation more than do other families.

Most people interested in buying a home do not understand that their best interests are served when they make a substantial down payment. There are two reasons why this is true: (1) The more money you have of your own to finance your home, the less you need to borrow and the less interest you will be required to pay; (2) the more money you are able to put into your home yourself, the greater is your incentive to achieve *full* ownership as soon as possible.

Interest rates for mortgages depend on a variety of factors, including:

1. Your credit standing.
2. The amount of money you are able to put into a down payment.
3. The area in which you live.
4. The type of home financing plan you have.

Your local savings and loan association can give you complete information on interest rates, down payment requirements and the type of home financing plan best suited to your individual needs. These financial institutions have been rendering specialized home financing assistance to four generations of American citizens. Consult one of their officers for complete information.

How to accumulate a down payment

You may find that buying a home at the present moment is just too expensive for you. But wait: this is not the end; it's the beginning.

Look at your monthly obligations to see if your expenses can be lowered. If they can (and they probably can), start a systematic savings program at your savings and loan association or a cooperative bank, aimed at building a fund for buying a home in the future.

Call it your "Home Ownership Fund." Add something to it each month, however small. You'll be amazed at how rapidly scattered nickels, dimes and quarters can build up.

Everyone in your family will get tremendous satisfaction from watching your Home Ownership Fund in a local savings association mature into a real down payment. Make it a family project by setting a target date. You may be able to achieve your goal long before—once all members of the family become interested in the fund.

Other initial costs of home ownership

You should choose your lending institution with great care. Often the savings and loan association where you built up your home ownership fund will protect you from mistakes you might otherwise make. Such an organization will, for instance, help you analyze your financial situation to make sure you can afford the house you want.

When you buy a home, other "first costs" are involved:

1. Appraisal fee and loan closing costs.
2. Fee for recording mortgage. By law, every deed or

mortgage must be recorded in the county where the property is located.

3. Legal fees and/or fees for title insurance or for obtaining evidence of good title to the property.

4. Insurance and taxes. Most institutions will add these costs to your mortgage payment and accumulate such funds for you so that these bills can be paid when due.

5. Any repair, modernization or landscaping work you feel is necessary to make the house suit your family's individual needs.

Insurance protects your investment

Of course you will want to carry fire insurance to cover the replacement value of your house, and you should cover yourself for the period between the time you buy it and when you actually move in. You also want protection from lightning, water damage, wind or hail, theft, and for your living expenses somewhere else if a disaster forces you to move out for awhile. And you will need liability insurance in case a workman, tradesman, friend or stranger has an accident on your premises.

You've reached the "end of the beginning"

With your first monthly mortgage payment, you begin to pay back the money loaned to you to buy your home. Besides this sum, called the "principal," you pay interest—payment for use of other people's money.

Remember that a home is the largest single purchase the typical family makes. If you're ready to buy, get all the advice you can about home financing. Choose a responsible thrift and home financing institution and you'll be certain of getting friendly, helpful and reliable advice.

Savings accounts

As you can see, the first form of investment for an American family is a savings account. No matter where you live in the United States you will find a savings and loan association; more likely than not, it is within a couple of blocks of where you work or live.

Many types of savings accounts are available at your savings and loan association. The passbook account has proved most popular over the years.

Why choose a passbook account at a savings and loan association over some other avenue of investment? For flexibility and simplicity. Here are some of the many advantages for the average American family with a passbook savings account:

1. You can add or withdraw funds as you please. Earnings may be retained in the account to compound, or may be paid out to you regularly.

2. The money in your account is free from speculative risk and the unpredictable ups and downs of the stock market. Any association investment is legally required to be a secure kind, such as government securities.

3. You always know your balance at a glance and can easily tabulate what your savings have earned or how much you need to complete your goal.

4. No huge minimum balance is needed to qualify you for the generous rate paid on passbook savings.

5. You can take out your money whenever you want. There are no restrictions.

6. You need not lock up savings for a long period to earn a good rate of return.

7. Passbook savings earn the current rate, whereas many certificates of deposit pay you less than the advertised yield if redeemed prior to the term stated on the certificate.

You can own savings accounts in a number of different ways, depending on your family needs.

1. *Individual ownership.* The account is in your name alone. It is completely under your control during your lifetime. At death, the balance in the account will be distributed by the executor of your will, according to its terms. If you have no will, the money will be distributed according to the inheritance laws of your state.

2. *Minor ownership.* Children can be account owners and may withdraw money when they can sign their names for identification purposes. Minors may also hold ownership in their own names but subject to withdrawal upon court order only. This kind of ownership is usually the result of an inheritance or the award of damages by a court.

3. *Joint tenancy ownership with right of survivorship.* You may hold this kind of account in your name and the names of any others you want as joint owners. A typical arrangement is to have an account issued in the name of husband and wife. For withdrawals, you may specify that either of you may take out money without the signature of the other, or you may want the signature of both to be required. Upon the death of a joint owner, his interest terminates and the account becomes the sole property of the survivor Joint ownership sometimes is held by three people.

4. *Tenancy in common ownership.* Ownership is in your name and the names of any others you may want as owners. The signatures of all parties to this account are required for a withdrawal. In the event of the death of an owner, his interest in the account passes to his estate.

5. *Individual trust ownership.* In an individual trust you may act as trustee for designated beneficiaries, such as your spouse or child. You alone may handle the account, including withdrawals and the changing of any or all beneficiaries. When the trust ends, after a stated number of years or at your death, the account may be payable to your designated beneficiaries. Trust accounts are governed by terms of the specific agreements establishing them.

6. *Co-trustee ownership.* You may open a savings account with another person and both of you may then act as co-trustees for designated beneficiaries. Each trustee may have the right to withdraw funds. You may appoint beneficiaries or change them as you wish. If one trustee should die, the surviving trustee may have sole control. After a stated number of years, or upon the death of both trustees, the balance of the account may be payable to beneficiaries.

123

7. *Fiduciary ownership.* As a guardian, executor or administrator, you may hold funds for some other person or persons. Acting in this capacity you may control the funds and you are responsible to the court of jurisdiction.

More than 73 percent of all savings associations—holding 96.4 percent of the total assets of the institutions—are members of the Federal Savings and Loan Insurance Corporation, an agency of the United States government. In these insured associations, each savings account is insured up to $15,000. Actually, families can maintain balances far in excess of $15,000 and still be fully insured, when they use combinations of accounts.

How certificate accounts work

In addition to the regular passbook accounts, many savings and loan associations are now offering savings certificates. These savings certificates are for terms of six months, twelve months or more. The minimum opening balance is $1,000. The certificates pay a "premium rate" (more than the regular passbook rate). Since plans vary, check with your association to find out more about its certificate plan.

A look at a savings and loan association

A savings and loan association is a "money store." The association "buys" the money in its savings department from customers like you. It pays you "rent" for the use of your money. The association "sells" its money through the loan department to people who want to buy homes of their own. While oversimplified, this is the basic operation of a savings and loan association.

Frequently, the first thing you notice as you enter the association is the teller area. The savings department transactions are taken care of here. At the teller counters you make deposits or withdrawals from your account as you please. In many associations, the teller counters also provide a place where you can make your mortgage payments if you prefer to pay in person rather than by mail.

Near the teller counters you will find the new accounts desks. These are manned by men and women experienced in all phases of savings accounts, budgeting, etc. They will not only advise you on what kinds of accounts to open, but during the course of your business with the association they can serve as savings advisers to you and your family.

Next, you will probably see the loan department. This is the "selling" section of the money store. Here a loan officer will talk with you about the mortgage loan you are seeking. He will want the location and description of the property you plan to buy and he will want some credit information about you (income, present indebtedness, references, etc.).

The next step is having an appraisal made of the house and property. This is usually done by a qualified appraiser from the association. After this, a loan committee determines how much can be loaned to you, and you are then notified. If the loan is satisfactory to you, arrangements are made for the loan closing—the time when you receive your trust deed or mortgage loan.

Other departments you will see in an average association might be the property improvement loan department. Here you can borrow money to add a room, put in a new kitchen, reroof the house or make any of a hundred home improvements.

Many associations maintain savings bond departments where you can purchase U.S. government savings bonds. While not a large part of savings and loan activity, the bond centers exist as a service to customers and to the government.

A number of associations have safety deposit vaults where you can store valuable papers, jewelry and other items you might want to keep under lock and key.

The savings and loan association is a local "one-stop" thrift institution. Virtually anything that has to do with your thrift or home ownership needs can be handled under one roof.

The savings and loan association can go a long way to stretch your dollar by giving you top earnings on the money you save, and by giving you many new ideas to stretch your dollar even further than you are doing now.

Visit your local association. Meet the people there. You will find them well worth your while.

POINTS TO REMEMBER

1. One of the best investments for the average American family is a savings account. Each account is insured for up to $15,000. Wherever you live in the U.S., you'll find a savings and loan association that will open a passbook account which, for flexibility and simplicity, serves you best.

2. Once you've built up a "Home Ownership Fund" in your savings account, you can make another good investment—your own home.

3. Make a substantial down payment. Less borrowing means less interest to pay.

4. Your savings and loan association remains your best dollar-stretcher, advising you on mortgages and other kinds of money management—to make all your dollars go further for you.

If you would like extra copies of How to Stretch Your Dollar for other members of your family or for gifts, order them by sending in these handy coupons:

How to Stretch Your Dollar
The Benjamin Company, Inc.
485 Madison Avenue
New York, New York 10022

Please send me_____copies. I enclose $1.00 for each copy of the book.

NAME_____

ADDRESS_____

CITY_____STATE_____ZIP_____

Please send me_____copies. I enclose $1.00 for each copy of the book.

NAME_____

ADDRESS_____

CITY_____STATE_____ZIP_____

Please send me_____copies. I enclose $1.00 for each copy of the book.

NAME_____

ADDRESS_____

CITY_____STATE_____ZIP_____